EXPLORING
PHILIP PULLMAN'S

HIS DARK
MATERIALS

Also by Lois H. Gresh

Dragonball Z
The Truth Behind a Series of Unfortunate Events
The Science of Supervillains
The Science of Superheroes
The Termination Node
Chuck Farris and the Tower of Darkness
Chuck Farris and the Labyrinth of Doom
Chuck Farris and the Cosmic Storm
Technolife 2020
The Computers of Star Trek
The Science of Anime
The Science of James Bond
The Fan's Guide to the Spiderwick Chronicles

EXPLORING PHILIP PULLMAN'S
HIS DARK MATERIALS

An Unauthorized Adventure Through *The Golden Compass, The Subtle Knife,* and *The Amber Spyglass*

LOIS H. GRESH

ST. MARTIN'S GRIFFIN ⚜ NEW YORK

EXPLORING PHILIP PULLMAN'S *HIS DARK MATERIALS*.
Copyright © 2007 by Lois H. Gresh. All rights reserved.
Printed in the United States of America. No part of this book may be used or
reproduced in any manner whatsoever without written permission except in the
case of brief quotations embodied in critical articles or reviews. For information,
address St. Martin's Press, 175 Fifth Avenue, New York, N.Y. 10010.

www.stmartins.com

Library of Congress Cataloging-in-Publication Data

Gresh, Lois H.
    Exploring Philip Pullman's His dark materials : an unauthorized adventure
through The golden compass, The subtle knife, and The amber spyglass / Lois
Gresh.—1st ed.
        p. cm.
    ISBN-13: 978-0-312-34743-7
    ISBN-10: 0-312-34743-X
    1. Pullman, Philip, 1946– His dark materials.   2. Young adult fiction,
English—History and criticism.   3. Fantasy fiction, English—History and
criticism.   I. Title

PR6066.U44 H564
823'.914—dc22   2005044617

First Edition: November 2007

10   9   8   7   6   5   4   3   2   1

To Philip Pullman,
who wrote one of the greatest trilogies of all time.
His Dark Materials is a masterpiece.

CONTENTS

PREFACE

This book was initially conceived as a young adult title, meaning it would appeal primarily to readers between the ages of approximately nine and fourteen years old. If you've read the *His Dark Materials* trilogy, then you know that the books are "serious" reads for young adults, and let's face it, they're "serious" reads for grown-ups, as well. The three books—*The Golden Compass*, *The Subtle Knife*, and *The Amber Spyglass*—appeal to mature readers of all ages.

While writing this book, I decided to take some liberty in exploring the topics of *His Dark Materials*. I offer conjectures, which are my own opinions about some of these "serious" subjects, but mostly I quote sources who know far more than I do about religion, God, heaven, hell, and quantum physics. I am, by no means, an authority on these topics, and frankly, anyone who claims to *know* what's really in hell and heaven has a lot of explaining to do.

This book delves into the *subjects* behind *His Dark Materials*. As such, it is not a book about the story lines and subplots, the characterization, and the writing style in *His Dark Materials*. Instead, the focus is on angels, souls, the afterlife, Dust, dark matter, and quantum entanglement: the meat of the books.

I usually avoid providing synopses of books, but in this case, I provide brief summaries in Chapter 1. If you haven't read *His Dark Materials*, I urge you to go to the library or bookstore, get these books, and read them right away. These three books will make you think a lot about what it means to be human, to have a soul and a conscience, what it means to do the right thing; and basically, the books will excite you with the thrill of adventure. The plots are full of adventure, twists and turns, battles, evil beings, angels, witches, and worlds of fun and fear.

PART I

FRONT MATTER

WHAT IS **HIS DARK MATERIALS**?

The simplest way of answering this question is to state that *His Dark Materials* is a trilogy of young adult fantasy novels. However, this is much too simple a description of Philip Pullman's *The Golden Compass* (Book 1), *The Subtle Knife* (Book 2), and *The Amber Spyglass* (Book 3).

In reality, *His Dark Materials* is an epic coming-of-age trilogy that includes vast sweeps of science, theology, and magic, while speculating about topics as profound as the meaning of life and the fundamental nature of God, Satan, and hell.

Sound like a young adult fantasy series to you?

Not exactly. . . .

Yet millions of children and teenagers are big fans of *His Dark Materials*. And so are their parents. This may be part of the reason Pullman is the first author to win two of England's prestigious Whitbread Awards for one book, *The Amber Spyglass*, which won the Children's Book award and also the top prize, the Book of the Year award.

But nothing is ever simple when talking about Philip Pullman's *His Dark Materials*, and as with the simple description of the series, mere popularity among readers isn't the key to winning the Whitbread Book of the Year Award. Much more is involved in the selection.

Juggling topics such as millions of parallel universes, quantum physics, and the existence of angels and witches, Pullman manages to write complex, nonstop action plots filled with unforgettable characters who are deeply drawn and deeply moving.

According to Pullman, as quoted on his official Web site, he thinks of the trilogy as "stark realism" not as fantasy. In fact, he says that he doesn't like fantasy. "The only thing about fantasy that interested me when I was writing this was the freedom to invent imagery such as the daemon; but that was only interesting because I could use it to say something truthful and realistic about human nature."[1]

Pullman further explains that *His Dark Materials* depicts "a struggle: the old forces of control and ritual and authority, the forces which have been embodied throughout human history in such phenomena as the Inquisition, the witch-trials, the burning of heretics, and which are still strong today. . . ."[2]

In 1985, Oxford University Press published Pullman's third novel (the first two were fairly unsuccessful), *The Ruby in the Smoke*. His editor, David Fickling, loved the book and claimed it was "as good as Wilkie Collins."[3]

Following the success of *The Ruby in the Smoke* came 1995's *Northern Lights*, later to be called *The Golden Compass*. This was the first book of a trilogy that Pullman called *His Dark Materials*. The book focuses on questions about the meaning of life and its

1. http://www.randomhouse.com/features/pullman.
2. Ibid.
3. Robert McCrum, Guardian Unlimited Books, January 27, 2002, as reported at http://books.guardian.co.uk/whitbread2001/story/0,11169,640032,00.html.

purpose, the nature of evil and good, how we should conduct ourselves, what really matters, and what doesn't matter at all. These powerful themes form the backbone of adventures of galactic proportions.

In 1995, Pullman won a Carnegie Prize for the book, and shortly after, when J. K. Rowling rose to conquer the literary scene, Pullman's book was published in the United States, as well as in France and Germany. Although *Northern Lights*, aka *The Golden Compass*, was published by the Oxford University Press as a children's book, it was published in the United States as an adult book. Pullman followed the success of *The Golden Compass*[4] with the final two books in the trilogy, *The Subtle Knife* in 1997 and *The Amber Spyglass* in 2000.

So enough prelude: What are these books *about*?

The Golden Compass takes place in a world that is much like our Earth, but there are differences. For example, it begins in Oxford, England, but the most powerful college is Jordan College rather than Oxford University. Jordan College is the leading research institution in the field of experimental theology which, loosely defined, means: quantum physics. But oddly enough, much of the science of *The Golden Compass* is from the late 1800s rather than from the late 1900s or early twenty-first century.

So right away, we know that we're in a different kind of Earth from the one we live in. The big clues, however, come in the form of daemons, soul creatures that people must keep with them at all times. These daemons are shapeshifters, meaning they can assume the forms of many different animals; yet while the daemons change form during a person's childhood, the creatures assume a fixed appearance as soon as the child reaches puberty. If a human

---

4. For the sake of convenience, I'll refer to *Northern Lights* aka *The Golden Compass* simply as *The Golden Compass* throughout this book.

dies, so does his daemon. If a daemon dies, the human might as well be dead, for he no longer has any soul or passion.

In addition to the daemons, *The Golden Compass* introduces the notion of witches, talking bears, and other life-forms.

From the opening pages, we know that this Earth is a stifling, scary place, dominated by a Church that subjects people to Inquisition-like terror. In fact, the Church in *The Golden Compass* feels like ultra-conservative Christianity pushed to the extreme.

As the book opens, main character Lyra Belacqua hides with her daemon, Pantalaimon, behind an armchair in the Retiring Room at Jordan College. Pantalaimon is in the form of a moth. The Master of Jordan College, with his raven daemon in tow, enters the Retiring Room and pours white powder into a decanter of special 1898 Tokay. Lord Asriel, expected soon from a long trip to the far North, will drink that Tokay and die. Lyra and Pan, as she calls her daemon, argue about what to do.

Lord Asriel arrives with his daemon, the snow leopard Stelmaria, who tells him to rest from his long journey. Lord Asriel tells the Scholars that he went to the far North to learn what happened to the missing Grumman expedition. He displays a series of photograms that he took in the far North, and these images show men with glowing particles on them called Dust. The images also show children who seem to be only partly there. In other images, everything is bathed in the Northern Lights, or the Aurora. Indeed, it appears that embedded in the Aurora is a city in a parallel universe. A lot has happened in this exciting novel, and we're only on page 23 of the book.

To summarize more quickly, we soon learn that Lord Asriel is performing weird research into the Dust and the parallel universe. He plans to return North, and Lyra begs him to let her go, but he refuses.

Lyra stays behind, and as she romps around the city with her friend Roger, she discovers that mysterious Gobblers are eating children, or so goes the gossip. The missing children never return, and soon Lyra discovers that a seductive woman is abducting them by unknown means. The woman's name is Mrs. Coulter, and she tries to befriend Lyra with offers of teenage luxuries.

Lyra is destined to change the world, we learn, but she must fulfill her destiny by making her own choices. She sets off on adventures with help from the gyptians (gypsies, we assume), whose children have been eaten by the Gobblers. Lyra and the gyptians head to the far North to search for the Gobblers and the lost children. They've heard stories that the children's disappearances have something to do with the Dust.

Of much help to Lyra is the strange alethiometer device, a golden compass. Only Lyra can read and interpret the symbols on the device, and she uses it to ask questions and receive instructions and explanations. The alethiometer even tells Lyra things about the future.

Lyra is kidnapped several times, she finds a few of the missing children, and she makes a good friend in the form of a talking bear named Iorek Byrnison. Iorek is an overthrown, sad, would-be bear king, whose title was taken from him by a human-wannabe bear called Iofur Raknison. Because bears don't have daemons, the wannabe Iofur carries a daemon doll—clearly, he's not fit to rule the ferocious and mighty bear kingdom.

At the end of *The Golden Compass*, Lord Asriel—who, as it happens, is Lyra's father—wants to find the source of the Dust in a parallel world. He tells Lyra that there are billions of parallel worlds, that the witches have known about the parallel worlds forever, that we can see these worlds through the Northern Lights, and that the Church excommunicates anyone who believes in the parallel worlds and in the Dust. He wants to destroy the notion of death.

Lyra sees Lord Asriel with Mrs. Coulter—who, as it happens, is Lyra's mother—on a bridge leading to the parallel world. Lord Asriel has done something cataclysmic to open that bridge, and now he intends to cross. He tells Mrs. Coulter that everyone will want to cross the bridge, that the end of the Church is near, that he will destroy all the Dust. It so happens that Mrs. Coulter, the Church, and the General Oblation Board (GOB in Gobblers) all want to destroy the Dust, too. Which makes Lyra think. . . .

Perhaps the Dust is good rather than evil. After all, if the adults in the world think Dust is evil, then it must be good stuff. So Lyra and Pan walk across the bridge into the other world.

And by doing so, they walk into the second book in the trilogy, *The Subtle Knife*.

This book begins with the story of twelve-year-old Will Parry, the son of an Arctic explorer who disappeared long ago. Will is the sole caretaker of an emotionally damaged mother. Will shops, cleans, cooks, and tries to help his mother cope with her imaginary enemies who, she claims, break into the house and demand things from her. Finally, when men really do break into the house, seeking his father's exploration notes, Will arranges for his piano teacher to take care of his mother, and he flees, accidentally killing one of the men during his escape. Filled with remorse about killing a man, Will simultaneously worries about his mother and wonders who will feed the cat.

Will stumbles across a window—a tear in space—in his version of Oxford, England (not Lyra's version of Oxford, England), and stepping through it, enters another world in a city called Cittàgazze.

Here, he hooks up with Lyra, her daemon, and her alethiometer. It seems that, in this new world, specters are killing all the adults, and hordes of crazed children roam the streets.

Along comes witch Serafina Pekkala, who must save her fellow witches from torture at the hands of Mrs. Coulter. It seems that Lyra's mother is still trying to find her . . . for evil purposes, no doubt.

In addition to Serafina Pekkala, Aeronaut Lee Scoresby also tries to help Lyra and Will uncover the truth behind the specters and the Dust. Scoresby flies off to find Stanislaus Grumman, who is not only an Arctic explorer but also a shaman. Lyra's mother, Mrs. Coulter, is still on the prowl for her, intending no good; and Lyra meets Dr. Mary Malone, a researcher of Dust who calls her field theoretical physics rather than theological magic. A strange and evil man named Sir Charles Latrom sends Will and Lyra on a quest to find a magic knife, which we later know as the subtle knife.

Apparently, Cittàgazze is a crossroads among all the billions of worlds, yet no adults can enter Cittàgazze because of the specters. And apparently, the entire system of worlds is in turbulence, with disturbances everywhere, as if the balance of nature is horribly askew.

As Lyra is the only person who can truly interpret the symbols of the alethiometer and read the future, Will is the only person who can wield the subtle knife, which cuts windows from one world to the next. The knife also cuts through all materials, a characteristic that proves extremely useful when satanic evils are chasing you from world to world.

At the end, Lyra's alethiometer tells her that she must help Will find his father, the Arctic explorer; we know that two forces are preparing for an enormous battle; and Lyra is kidnapped once again.

At this point, we begin the third book, *The Amber Spyglass*, in which Will is determined to save Lyra, and he enlists the aid of angels and bear king Iorek Byrnison. Meanwhile Dr. Mary Malone has left her world for another, where she encounters the humorous *mulefa* creatures.

In the third book, *The Amber Spyglass*, the subtle knife breaks, and Lord Asriel's Gallivespian spies (tiny creatures) accompany Will and Lyra on their adventurers. One of these adventures leads the group to the Land of the Dead.

The Church sends an assassin priest to kill Lyra, the vile harpies learn a lesson, and all sorts of people and creatures try to help Lyra and Will save the billions of worlds from destruction. We see talking bears, witches, angels, Lord Asriel, and even God (somewhat shriveled and glad to be done with it all).

Mary Malone constructs an amber spyglass to help her see the Dust, and in the end, only love can set you free.

Now, this book—the one you're reading—attempts to analyze some of the main elements in *His Dark Materials*.

- Chapter 2 analyzes the science and philosophy of Dust. Just what might it be? And what does it have to do with dark matter, consciousness, and sin (Adam and Eve)? This chapter is very straightforward and serious; the topics of Dust and dark matter are based in science and philosophy, and hence cannot be treated lightly or quickly.
- Chapter 3 discusses angels, gods, and paradise.
- Chapter 4 is about witches.
- Chapter 5 focuses on daemons and souls.
- Chapter 6 discusses parallel worlds.
- Chapter 7 focuses on the afterlife, with subjects such as hell, harpies, heaven, and the world of the dead.
- Chapter 8 delves into the ideas behind specters, vampires, night ghasts, and zombies.
- Chapter 9 describes the role of the Aurora Borealis (Northern Lights).
- Chapter 10 is the first Weird Science section and describes the alethiometer, Lodestone Resonator, mechanical insects, zeppelins, and gyrocopters.

- Chapter 11 is the second Weird Science section and describes strange topics, such as the *I Ching* and shamanism.

As you can see from this lineup, the focus is on the scientific and philosophical ideas in *His Dark Materials*. As for science, we tend to take for granted what's around us, such as toasters, ovens, cars, subways, and televisions. But to a visitor from another world—say, one of those billions of worlds in *His Dark Materials*—the things we take for granted are probably pretty strange. When Lyra visits Will's world, she's amazed by ordinary things such as cars, which don't exist in her world. And to Will, the alethiometer and the Dust seem magical. Taken to extremes, most of the science in *His Dark Materials* seems magical to us: billions of parallel worlds, dark matter, and quantum physics, to name only three.

As for philosophical ideas, we tend to take for granted that our religions are good; that those who fight religion may not be so good; that we probably won't be able to read the minds of our teachers, friends, neighbors, or parents; and that we're probably not going to encounter angels, harpies, witches, tiny people, and talking bears anytime soon. These ideas are all taken for granted in *His Dark Materials*. And of course, there's the Big One: daemons. In our world, Earth, our souls are inside us. In Lyra's world, souls are shapeshifting creatures who are born with you and die with you. They talk to their humans, and they change what they look like: turn into different creatures based on how their humans feel or what their humans are doing at any particular time. As soon as a child is about twelve years old (puberty), the daemon finds its permanent shape and never changes into another creature again.

When asked about his comment that *His Dark Materials* is "stark reality," Philip Pullman responds, "Well, when I made that comment I was trying to distinguish between these books and the kind of books most general readers think of as fantasy, the sub-Tolkien thing involving witches and elves and wizards and dwarves."[5] He further states that, "I'm telling a story about a realistic subject, but I'm using the mechanism of fantasy."[6]

What do you think he means? Is the stark realism about right versus wrong, religion, quantum physics, billions of worlds, or what?

Luckily, he tells us. As CNN reports, "There are, indeed, fantastical creations throughout the trilogy, but Pullman says he uses them to reflect certain truths about human nature. . . . In *The Golden Compass*, we meet daemons, the animal soul mates of humans in Lyra's world. Daemons can change form as long as their soul mates are children, but once they become adults, those creatures become fixed—a reflection of 'the inner nature of its human.'"[7] So the stark reality probably has to do with the truth about what it means to be human.

Philip Pullman is quoted by many sources as stating that *His Dark Materials* "lay in the extraordinary poetry of the phrase 'dark matter,' and my discovery that Milton had anticipated in *Paradise Lost*: 'Unless the Almighty Maker them ordain his dark materials to create more worlds.'"[8]

And so with that in mind, we move to our chapter about Dust, or dark matter. What is Dust? What is dark matter? And what do these things have to do with quantum physics and outer space?

5. Dave Welch, "Philip Pullman Reaches the Garden," an author interview at http://www.powells.com/authors/pullman.html.
6. Ibid.
7. Lili Ladaga, "Philip Pullman Weaves Spell with His Dark Materials," from an author interview by CNN Book News at http://archives.cnn.com/2000/books/news/11/10/philip.pullman/
8. Philip Pullman, "The Science of Fiction," http://www.hisdarkmaterials.org/; also see Lili Ladaga, CNN Book News, ibid.

DUS+, DARK MA++ER, DARK ENERGY, AND O+HER CELES+IAL +HINGS

Into this wild abyss,
The womb of nature and perhaps her grace,
Of neither sea, nor shore, nor air, nor fire,
But all of these in their pregnant causes mixed
Confusedly, and which thus must ever fight,
Unless the almighty maker them ordain
His dark materials to create more worlds,
Into this wild abyss the wary fiend
Stood on the brink of hell and looked a while,
Pondering his voyage . . . [9]

Part 1. Dust

It was the above excerpt from John Milton's *Paradise Lost* that gave Philip Pullman the title for his trilogy. In *His Dark Materials*, Dust is an unknown phenomenon that exists throughout the universe. It oozes across the boundaries between worlds (see Chapter 6, "Parallel Worlds"). It seeps through windows created by

9. Milton's *Paradise Lost*, Book Two.

Will's subtle knife. It billows around adults but is nonexistent around children. Dust is a central mystery in *His Dark Materials*: There are hints that Dust might be our consciousness, it might be linked to our souls; it might be a physical manifestation of adult love and intimacy; it might be sin; it might create the angels; it might be the stuff we call dark matter that constitutes a large portion of our universe.

In *The Golden Compass*, both Lord Asriel and Mrs. Coulter make it clear that they want to understand and control the Dust. Apparently, the control of everything by the highly conservative Church is based on Dust. Scholars in our real world (the one in which I'm writing this book) believe that the Dust in Lyra's world is the same as "the mysterious charged particles known in our world as dark matter."[10] The dark matter in our real world is invisible, and as far as we know today, confined to outer space. In *The Golden Compass*, scientists and Church clerics struggle to define Ruskakov particles (collectively called the Dust), which have only become visible due to technological advances. Further, in Lyra's world, the Dust is related to the sin of Adam and Eve. And as we read *The Subtle Knife* and *The Amber Spyglass*, it becomes clear that Pullman also intends us to ponder that the Dust is our human consciousness, a form of spiritual matter that exists everywhere throughout the universe. Somehow, this Dust opens our lives to alternate realities, or parallel worlds. Hence, while scholars (and I, a mere writer) do indeed believe that the Dust is dark matter, it's also clear that the Dust is far more.

As *The Golden Compass* opens, Lyra is spying on Lord Asriel's presentation to fellows of Jordan College in Oxford. He has a special lantern device that shows photograms to the audience.

10. For example, Michael Chabon in his essay, "Dust & Daemons," *The New York Review of Books*, Volume 51, Number 5, March 25, 2004, http://www.nybooks.com/articles/17000.

The first photogram merely shows an Arctic explorer in the moonlight. The second photogram is the same scene, but Lord Asriel explains that he took this second image with a "new specially prepared emulsion." This is a key moment in the first book, when the reader is first introduced to Dust:

"[The explorer] was bathed in light, and a fountain of glowing particles seemed to be steaming from his upraised hand.

"'That light,' said the Chaplain, 'is it going up or coming down?'

"'It's coming down,' said Lord Asriel, 'but it isn't light. It's Dust.'

"Something in the way he said it made Lyra imagine Dust with a capital letter, as if this wasn't ordinary Dust."[11]

Lord Asriel shows an additional photogram, also taken with the new emulsion, and this one shows a distant city flickering in the Northern Lights, or Aurora Borealis (see Chapter 9, "Aurora Borealis (Northern Lights)"). Clearly, it's odd to see a city flickering up in the sky. Clearly, the city is either not real or not of this world. And hence, the mystery of Dust begins.

The fellows of the College conclude that the city is from another world:

"'And now Lord Asriel has taken a picture of one of these other worlds,' the Librarian said. 'And we have funded him to go back and look for it. . . .'"[12]

Already, we assume that the Dust has something to do with the Aurora Borealis and with other worlds.

Later in the story, a mysterious and beautiful woman named Mrs. Coulter takes Lyra from Oxford to London, where she tries to interest the girl in high society. At one of Mrs. Coulter's posh parties, Lyra overhears people talking about the Dust. As a middle-aged man explains:

11. Philip Pullman, *The Golden Compass*. New York: Knopf, 1996, page 20.
12. Ibid., pp. 30–31.

"'It was discovered by a Muscovite . . . a man called Rusakov, and they're usually called Rusakov Particles after him. Elementary particles that don't interact in any way with others—very hard to detect, but the extraordinary thing is that they seem to be attracted to human beings . . . some human beings more than others. Adults attract it, but not children. At least, not much, and not until adolescence.'"[13]

So not only does the Dust have something to do with the Aurora Borealis and other worlds, it also is connected to elementary particles (a clear reference to the particles that physicists study), as well as what happens to children when they reach puberty. The clues are mounting, but so is the confusion: Just what are these elementary particles that relate to such diverse things?

Lyra soon learns that Mrs. Coulter is a founding member of the General Oblation Board. The General Oblation Board is part of the Church and performs unknown experiments on children and Dust. Naturally, this information frightens Lyra—she doesn't want the General Oblation Board to experiment on *her*!—and she decides to run away, quickly, from Mrs. Coulter.

And then, as she's about to escape, she hears a Bishop saying that the "last experiments confirmed what I always believed—that Dust is an emanation from the dark principle itself, and . . . what used to be a heresy. . . ."[14]

Adding to the mystery of Dust is this new piece of information, that it is connected to heresy against the Church and is directly related to a "dark principle," leading us to believe the Bishop might be referring to sin.

Astute readers probably infer at this point (I didn't) that the Dust is all of the above and that it is dark matter, which we'll talk about soon. If the universe was created from original, pure,

13. Ibid., pp. 88–89.
14. Ibid., pp. 95–96.

"good" matter a long time ago, then how did evil arise? Could the evil be the dark matter itself, the sin? Again, I did not gather this much so soon in *The Golden Compass*. I was well into the novel before I started figuring out what Pullman was getting at.

And as the novel progresses, the issues surrounding Dust become more complex. Lord Asriel goes to the far North to build a bridge to the city he has discovered in the sky. He figures that the Dust is falling from a parallel world, and he intends to find the source of the Dust and discover its secrets.

Lyra follows Lord Asriel to the far North, and it seems that she is also poised to enter this parallel world with him. When she asks about the world he sees in the Aurora Borealis, he explains that the world is "One of uncountable billions of parallel worlds. . . . And I'm going to that world beyond the Aurora . . . because I think that's where all the Dust in the universe comes from."[15]

The puzzle thickens yet more when we consider the role of "daemons" (see Chapter 5, "Daemons") in the Dust mystery. In Lyra's world, everyone has a daemon, which is an animal of the opposite sex (Lyra's Pantalaimon is a male daemon) that stays with the person throughout life. The daemons are shapeshifters, which means they can look like a cat one minute, then look like a mouse the next. However, once the person becomes an adolescent, the daemon can no longer change shapes. Rather, it becomes fixed: as a cat, a mouse, a dove, a hawk, a tiger, etc. And when the daemon settles into a permanent animal avatar, representing the person's true character, that's when Dust starts to settle on the person.

Lord Asriel asks Lyra to read from Genesis in the Bible; in particular, he points her to the forbidden fruit scene with Adam and Eve. In Lyra's world, paradise is where Adam and Eve are children, just like Lyra, who have shapeshifting daemons. In Lyra's world,

15. Ibid., p. 376.

when Adam and Eve eat the forbidden fruit, their daemons assume fixed, adult forms; sin is born, as well as shame and death. And given that we're all "dust to dust," the cosmic Dust arises from this original sin and the settling of daemons into fixed, adult form.

As for Dust being consciousness, *The Golden Compass* introduces the notion that, in Lyra's world, savage Tartars are "trepanning" themselves so they can absorb extra Dust. This implies that the Dust is evil. In our real world (the one in which you're reading this book), people used trepanning in ancient times to give them cosmic consciousness. Let's not tiptoe around the subject: Trepanning means that people use a trephine on their skulls to remove a disk or cylindrical core from it. The trephine is a surgical instrument that cuts circular sections from the skull. (For more about this subject, see Chapter 11, "Weird Science, Part 2.")

The connection between Dust and cosmic consciousness is enforced by the notion that only Lyra can read the future and get advice from the alethiometer (see Chapter 10, "Weird Science, Part 1"). The truth-telling device, she assumes, may be driven by the Dust. At the end of *The Golden Compass*, Lyra follows Lord Asriel over the bridge into the parallel world.

It's all very complex and smacks of religion and physics, right and wrong: intricate subjects for young adult readers and children. Do you remember in Chapter 1 when I told you that *His Dark Materials* was first published in England as a children's series, but that later, in the United States, it was published as adult fiction? Now you know why. These are subjects that are hard for most children to absorb. They're weighty topics for most adults. Yet it's the adventure, the ride, of the three novels, that carries kids through to the end. And the same is true for the adults: Everyone loves a good adventure.

The adventure continues with the second book, *The Subtle Knife*, as we're introduced to Will, who ultimately is Adam to Lyra's Eve. Setting aside Will's saga for now, as well as the complexities of the plots, subplots, and concluding third novel, we learn a lot about Dust in *The Subtle Knife*.

Lyra tracks down a theoretical physicist named Dr. Mary Malone, who works in a Dark Matter Research Unit. It's becoming very clear to us, the readers, that Dust is intimately tied to dark matter. When Lyra asks Dr. Malone to define dark matter, the physicist replies, "There's more stuff out there in the universe than we can see. . . . But no one can detect it. . . . Normally, they put detectors very deep underground, but what we've done instead is to set up an electromagnetic field around the detector that shuts out the things we don't want and lets through the ones we do. Then we amplify the signal and put it through a computer. . . . We call them shadow particles, shadows. . . . You know what? They're conscious. That's right. Shadows are particles of consciousness. . . . And here goes the crazy part: you can't see them unless you expect to. Unless you put your mind in a certain state."[16]

Because Lyra uses this certain state of mind to read the alethiometer, she knows how to use Dr. Malone's computer to produce shadow particle patterns. She can use her consciousness, her spiritual being, to communicate with the particles, the Dust, which form a stream of lights that remind her of the Aurora Borealis. Lyra also determines that the shadow particles contain important information. She wants Dr. Malone to program the computer so Lyra and the shadow particles can communicate in textual form on a screen.

This section of the book reinforces Pullman's idea that the Dust is the same as dark matter (the shadow particles), which is the same as our cosmic consciousness, which is tightly connected to daemons (possibly our souls), original sin, and billions of parallel worlds. The genius in Pullman's work is that we believe what he's telling us, we're captured by the fantasy and ad-

16. Philip Pullman, *The Subtle Knife*. New York: Knopf, 1997, page 88.

ventures, the images he creates; and we drink in the enormous complexity of *His Dark Materials* very easily.

Later, Dr. Malone discusses the Dust, or dark matter, with her research partner. She talks about the Big Bang:

"But suppose something happened thirty, forty thousand years ago. There were shadow particles before then, obviously—they've been around since the Big Bang—but there was no physical way of amplifying their effects at our level . . . the level of human beings. And then something happened, I can't imagine what, but it involved evolution. . . . Suddenly we became conscious."[17]

Everything is rolled together when Dr. Malone does program the computer to communicate using text. She asks questions of the shadow particles.

"Are you shadows? YES.

"Are you the same as Lyra's Dust? YES.

"And is that dark matter? YES.

"Dark matter is conscious? EVIDENTLY.

". . . human evolution? . . . CORRECT."[18]

In addition, the computer adds that Dust is also "angels" (see Chapter 3, "Angels, God, and Paradise"), and that this angel Dust is designed to give consciousness to humans, to awaken them to their destiny. In this case, human destiny is to join an angelic rebellion against the Authority, whom we take to mean God himself.

Mrs. Coulter heads to the far North to try to eliminate the Dust from the universe. After all, the Dust is original sin, and the Church doesn't like sin. The method used to eliminate Dust, or sin, is to cut a child's daemon (soul) from him before he becomes a teenager.[19] The Church calls this process "inter-

---

17. Ibid., p. 238.
18. Ibid., p. 248.
19. My thanks here to Alice Turner for pointing out that *coulter* means *cutter*, as in cutting off the child's daemon.

cision" and carries it out under the authority of the General Oblation Board, of which Mrs. Coulter is now chairman. Worse, Mrs. Coulter sends out child snatchers known as Gobblers (related, perhaps, to the General Oblation Board—GOB?) to kidnap children so Mrs. Coulter can perform the hideous intercisions. Once a child loses its daemon, the child loses its soul.

Now, plenty of articles have been written about Pullman's take on organized religion and the Church, so we're not going to take sides here, we're not going to delve much into the issues surrounding *His Dark Materials* and religion.[20] Rather, our focus is on Dust, dark matter, angels, daemons, witches, and parallel worlds, among other interesting topics. We leave the religious debate to those who are more knowledgeable about religious matters.

With his theories about Dust, Philip Pullman brilliantly explores one of today's hottest scientific topics: dark matter. In fact, in 2003, *Scientific American* published a special report called *Does Dark Matter Really Exist?* And as you'll read very soon, scientists are exploring the notion that dark matter indeed is tied to the Big Bang and our human consciousness.

Part 2. Dark Matter

> The discovery by Zwicky (1933) that visible matter accounts for only a tiny fraction of all the mass in the universe may turn out to have been one of the most profound new insights produced by scientific exploration during the twentieth century.
> —Sidney van den Bergh, *The Early History of Dark Matter*[21]

20. The astute reader may guess that Pullman dislikes organized religion, believes in free will of humans, and does not favor the thought that we're all ruled by God, the Church, and Satan.
21. Sidney van den Bergh, *The Early History of Dark Matter*. The Astronomical Society of the Pacific, June 1999, p. 1.

"Of all the many mysteries of modern astronomy, none is more vexing than the nature of dark matter," writes Mordehai Milgrom in his *Scientific American* article, "Ninety-Five Percent of the Universe Has Gone Missing. Or Has It?" Dr. Milgrom is professor of theoretical physics at the Weizmann Institute in Rehovot, Israel. He writes that the dark matter "problem arose because of a mismatch in the masses of galaxies and larger cosmic structures."[22]

The components of galaxies include stars and gas; of galaxy clusters, gas and galaxies. The components move but are held by gravitational pull. Physics and math equations tell us how much mass must be present in the universe to create the required gravitational pull. However, the equations don't balance: They indicate that there's a lot more mass in the universe than we can tally in the known mass structures. As Dr. Milgrom writes, "Dark matter is the only explanation that astronomers can conjure up for the various mass discrepancies, if we cleave to the accepted laws of physics."[23]

Astronomers and physicists estimate that 90 or more percent of the mass of the universe is really dark matter, which does not seem to radiate any light. Others estimate that 5 percent of the universe's mass is ordinary, visible matter such as protons and neutrons,[24] 25 percent is dark matter, and the remaining 70 percent is something called dark energy. Regardless of the exact per-

22. Mordehai Milgrom, "Ninety-Five Percent of the Universe Has Gone Missing. Or Has It?" *Scientific American* special report, *Does Dark Matter Really Exist?*, 2003, p. 3.
23. Ibid., p. 4.
24. According to Michio Kaku on page 11 of his January 2005 book, *Parallel Worlds* (New York: Doubleday), "the WMAP satellite showed that the visible matter we see around us (including the mountains, planets, stars, and galaxies) makes up a paltry 4 percent of the total matter and energy content of the universe. . . . Most of the universe is actually made up of mysterious, invisible material of totally unknown origin. The familiar elements that make up our world constitute only 0.03 percent of the universe. . . . [T]he universe is dominated by entirely new, unknown forms of matter and energy."

centages, it's clear to most scientists that dark matter and dark energy make up most of the matter in the universe. What's unclear is the composition of the dark matter, what it really *is*.

"All sorts of suggestions have been proposed," writes Dr. James Kaler, professor of astronomy at the University of Illinois at Champaign-Urbana, "from weird atomic particles through unobserved black holes to neutrinos (the near-massless particles created in atomic reactions) released during the Big Bang, the creation event of the universe." Dr. Kaler further speculates that dark matter might consist of dim red or brown dwarf stars.[25] Other scientists speculate that dark matter could be made up of black holes, white dwarfs, or "massive quantities of small particles, like WIMPs, axions, or strange quark nuggets; and [there are] more exotic speculations, like mirror matter or cosmic Q-balls."[26] Don't worry, I'll tell you a bit about these possibilities later in this chapter. But for now, let's stick to some basics:

The Chandra X-ray Observatory of Harvard University tells us that 95 percent of the universe is invisible to us and most likely consists of three components. The first is ordinary matter, such as protons, neutrons, and the molecules that are in plants, animals, the Earth, and cosmic entities such as other planets, moons, and so forth. The second type of matter is the dark matter, which we can't see at any wavelength, including visible light, radio, infrared, optical, ultraviolet, and gamma-ray telescope.[27] And the third type is dark energy, which I'll discuss later in this chapter.

25. James Kaler, *Extreme Stars at the Edge of Creation*. New York: Cambridge University Press, 2001, p. 45.
26. Tom Siegfried, *Strange Matters: Undiscovered Ideas at the Frontiers of Space and Time*. Washington, D.C.: Joseph Henry Press, 2002, p. 88.
27. Chandra X-ray Observatory, Harvard University. http://chandra.harvard.edu/resources/faq/dmatter/dmatter-12.html.

Basically, reports Harvard, 70 percent of the universe is dark energy, while 25 percent is dark matter, and only 5 percent is ordinary matter.[28]

As you might have guessed, nobody really knows much about dark matter. Speculation began in the 1930s, when Fritz Zwicky, an astronomy professor at the California Institute of Technology, detected weird behavior in the Coma Cluster, a collection of thousands of galaxies that are approximately 370 million light years from Earth. The galaxies were moving with a speed that didn't make sense to Dr. Zwicky, who concluded that they contained a lot of matter that astronomers were unable to see. As Brian Greene, professor of physics and mathematics at Columbia University, writes, "They were moving too quickly for their visible matter to muster an adequate gravitational force to keep them tethered to the group."[29] Dr. Zwicky determined that the Coma Cluster contained an enormous amount of dark matter. Researchers later agreed with his conclusion, as there seemed to be more mass in the Coma Cluster than astronomers could detect in the visible galaxy. Other than ordinary matter, something else was out there: the dark matter.

Then in 1936, Sinclair Smith at the Mount Wilson Observatory came to the same conclusion about the Virgo Cluster. There was a large amount of invisible dark matter exerting a gravitational pull significant enough to hold the galaxies together.

In 1939, Horace Babcock measured the spin of the outer region of the Andromeda galaxy. He determined that the "stars on Andromeda's outer edges appeared to revolve around the galaxy

28. Ibid.
29. Brian Greene, *The Fabric of the Cosmos: Space, Time, and the Texture of Reality*. New York: Alfred A. Knopf, 2004, p. 294.

much more rapidly than they should, based on simple applications of Newton's law of gravity."[30]

Then in the 1970s, astronomer Vera Rubin and her collaborators at the Carnegie Institute of Washington, proved that the visible galactic matter could not supply enough gravity to keep the stars within numerous spinning galaxies from breaking free of one another. They also showed that gravity would hold the stars together if the galaxies were submerged somehow in a large amount of dark matter. This dark matter, they postulated, would have a total mass that was much greater than that of the galaxy's ordinary, visible mass. Astronomers determined that the universe is made up of matter that does not form stars, hence providing light; that this matter exerts strong gravity upon cosmic structures; and that it is invisible.

And then, by the 1980s, astronomers felt that 90 percent of the mass in the galaxy is unseen and that dark matter exists in the vast regions between galaxies as well.

So by calculating the mass of all visible matter—stars and gas—in a galaxy, astronomers determine what the rotation speed of the galaxy is supposed to be. This is how they calculate the gravity of the matter to the galaxy. Because most galaxies rotate much faster than the equations indicate that they should be rotating—more than twice as fast—then, following Einstein's theory of gravity, galaxies should be flying apart. But the galaxies are not flying apart. We assume that Einstein's theory of gravity is accurate—it's been proven accurate in all other cases, so why should we suddenly assume a deviation?

According to Harvard University, X-ray telescopes have detected huge clouds of multimillion-degree gas in galaxy clusters. The clouds increase the mass of the clusters, but "not enough to

30. Tom Siegfried, op. cit., p. 88.

solve the mystery" of gravity and unknown mass in the universe. The X-ray telescope measures show that "there must be at least four times as much dark matter as all the stars and gas we observe, or the hot gas would escape the cluster."[31]

So what is this dark matter, or Dust in Lyra's world? Candidates include MACHOs, WIMPs, and hydrogen gas. The first, MACHOs, are Massive Compact Halo Objects and include white dwarfs, red dwarfs, brown dwarfs, neutron stars, and black holes. The WIMPs, or Weakly Interacting Massive Particles, are exotic subatomic particles such as massive neutrinos, axions, and photinos. And while it's unlikely that the dark matter is hydrogen gas, we'll discuss that theory as well.

As for MACHOs, some astronomers believe that dark matter is lurking in the outer regions of galaxies, that this dark matter is in the halos surrounding the galaxies, and that the dark matter is in the form of Massive Compact Halo Objects the size of small stars. Most MACHOs have approximately half the sun's mass, which means they might be burned-out stars called white dwarfs.

White dwarfs are condensed, final versions of small and medium stars. They're plentiful throughout the universe. The white dwarf is dim because of its size, not because it is cool. Though a typical white dwarf has half the sun's mass, it is only a little larger than Earth. What this means is that the white dwarf is one of the densest forms of matter. In fact, the smaller the dwarf, the higher its mass.

Plentiful as they are, according to some scientists, the galaxy cannot possibly contain enough white dwarfs to account for much of the halo matter.[32] In addition, large amounts of helium

31. Chandra X-ray Observatory, op. cit. http://chandra.harvard.edu/xray astro/dark matter2.html.
32. Tom Siegfried, op. cit., p. 36.

are produced when large numbers of white dwarfs are present, and scientists have not observed these vast amounts of helium.

Is it possible, as many scientists think, that the dark matter is made up of brown dwarfs or red dwarfs?

Brown dwarfs are stars with masses that are less than eight percent of the sun's mass. To shine, stars need a higher mass than that of the brown dwarf. To be defined as a star, a cosmic body must be a self-luminous sphere of gas that is supported by full thermonuclear fusion.[33]

The brown dwarf is basically a failed star that glows for a while after it is formed. The temporary glowing is caused by the heat from gravitational contraction: from a slight amount of thermonuclear fusion. While the brown dwarf tends to be larger than a planet, it's not big enough to generate enough internal pressure to explode into a star. Basically, the brown dwarf cools and shrinks with significant mass, and then disappears.

Some scientists say that brown dwarfs are "too small to be the MACHOs."[34] In addition, scientists have no evidence that our galaxy has enough brown dwarfs to account for the dark matter. As James Kaler writes, "The masses of bottom-end stars and brown dwarfs are so small that to make any impact on the dark matter problem, there would have to be huge numbers of them. . . . Deep examination of our Galaxy's halo by the Hubble Space Telescope shows . . . a remarkable absence of faint red dwarfs. If the trend continues, we might expect relatively few brown dwarfs, making these exceedingly dim stars yet harder to find."[35]

Red dwarfs are abundant in the universe and have a mass less than one-third of the sun's mass. The red dwarf emits very little light, and they slowly contract over long periods of time.

33. James Kaler, op.cit., p. 45.
34. Tom Siegfried, op. cit., p. 36.
35. James Kaler, op. cit., p. 45.

Scientists think that red dwarfs may be the most common stars in the universe. For example, the nearest star (Proxima Centauri) to the sun happens to be a red dwarf, as are twenty of the next thirty stars closest to the sun.

As for red dwarfs being dark matter, however, many scientists claim that red dwarfs "have been ruled out."[36] This may be because scientists cannot find many red dwarfs (see James Kaler's comment above).

Another type of MACHO is the neutron star, which according to NASA is "the imploded core of a massive star produced by a supernova explosion. According to astronomer . . . Frank Shu, 'A sugar cube of neutron-star stuff on Earth would weigh as much as all of humanity!'"[37] In fact, NASA scientists estimate that one sugar cube of neutron star material weighs about 100 million tons.[38] As the core of a star collapses, all of its protons and electrons are crushed together, and all the proton-electron pairs are turned into neutrons. When the neutrons stop the star from further collapse, a neutron star is born. This neutron star is extremely dense and compact, and has no empty space.

Alex Gary Markowitz of the University of California astronomy department claims that neutron stars "are probably not a major contributor to the dark matter mass."[39] And according to NASA, "These objects occur less frequently than white dwarfs. As a result of a supernova, a release of a massive amount of energy and heavy elements should occur. However, there is no such evidence that they occur in sufficient numbers in the halo of galaxies."[40]

And finally, in the category of MACHOs, we have black

36. Tom Siegfried, op. cit., p. 36.
37. http://imagine.gsfc.nasa.gov/docs/dict_jp.html#neutron_star.
38. http://imagine.gsfc.nasa.gov/docs/science/know_11/neutron_stars.html.
39. http://www.astro.ucla.edu/~agm/darkmtr.html.
40. http://imagine.gsfc.nasa.gov/docs/teachers/galaxies/imagine/page18.html.

holes. Is it possible that *these* MACHOs make up the dark matter in the universe?

First, let's explore for a moment how a star, any star, is born. A large amount of hydrogen and other gases begins to collapse due to gravitational forces. As the gas contracts, its atoms collide at increasing speeds, and the gas gets very hot. Eventually, the gas is so hot that the hydrogen atoms no longer bounce off each other. The hydrogen atoms start to combine into helium atoms. As the hydrogen atoms merge, enormous heat is released, much like the heat in a hydrogen bomb, and the star is born and begins to glow. The gas stops contracting because the heat increases the pressure of the gas, hence balancing the gas against the gravitational forces that are pushing it in. The star continues to shine.

As the star runs out of fuel, the hydrogen gas, it starts to cool. The loss of heat means that the pressure of the gas no longer balances against the gravitational push, and so the star begins to contract.

At some point, the gravitational push on the surface of the star bends the light inward. The light can no longer escape from the star, and the star begins to wink out.

A black hole is a star "that is sufficiently massive and compact [with] such a strong gravitational field that light is dragged in and cannot escape."[41] Assume that an enormous amount of matter is crushed by its own gravity. Further assume that nuclear fusion doesn't occur—in other words, there is no explosion. Because matter is crushed into such huge densities, spacetime is severely warped, and the spacetime warp itself has a strong gravitational force. If the force is powerful enough, a black hole is born.

The black hole has tremendous density. Its gravitational pull is so extreme that scientists simply infer that it exists by measur-

---

41. Stephen W. Hawking, *The Illustrated Theory of Everything*. Beverly Hills, CA: New Millennium Press, 2003, p. 30.

ing its pull on the gases swirling around it. A black hole usually has a mass of approximately four billion of our suns. The black hole tends to eat gaseous matter at the rate of a million suns per year or more.[42] If any matter reaches the edge of the black hole, which is called its event horizon, the black hole sucks in and swallows the matter. Light does not escape from the black hole.

Now, how likely is it that dark matter consists of black holes? The scientists at Harvard's Chandra X-ray Observatory conjecture that dark matter and black holes may *interact*. In other words, if the universe contains many black holes, as seems to be the case, then black holes must interact at some point with the "halo of dark matter that surrounds a galaxy like our own."[43] This in no way implies that dark matter consists of black holes.

In fact, Chandra continues by supposing that the dark matter particles might actually be sucked into the black holes. The black holes would then gain in mass and attract yet more dark matter.

It is thought by many astronomers that a supermassive black hole exists in the middle of each galaxy. This supermassive black hole has a mass that is less than one percent of the mass of the galaxy. Hence, it seems unlikely that black holes are the same as dark matter. Remember: Dark matter supposedly comprises 90 or more percent of the mass of the universe.

In addition, a case can be made against black holes being dark matter by noting that dark matter is everywhere: It is not located in some organized, lumped way around cosmic objects such as black holes. It is spread out across the universe.

Much as we'd like to know what dark matter is—a MACHO would have helped our cause—we still don't know. Is it possible

42. L. E. Lewis Jr., *Our Superstring Universe: Strings, Branes, Extra Dimensions, and Superstring-M Theory*. Lincoln, NE: iUniverse, Inc., 2003, p. 34.
43. http://chandra.harvard.edu/resources/faq/dmatter/dmatter-19.html.

that dark matter is made of WIMPs, or Weakly Interacting Massive Particles?

WIMPs may have been created during the Big Bang, when the universe was formed. Scientists conjecture that WIMPs, which include massive neutrinos, axions, and photinos, may have been created in the correct amounts and with the correct properties to constitute dark matter.

Neutrinos are the top candidate for dark matter. Neutrinos are categorized as hot dark matter, which doesn't mean that they're hotter than the sun, but rather, that they move extremely fast through outer space. Neutrinos are extremely light with a mass of near zero. Their charge is approximately neutral. Being so light and chargeless, they're able to travel at near the speed of light and cover vast distances very quickly. In fact, neutrinos pass through other forms of matter—including our bodies—very easily. Stars, including our sun, emit these neutral particles in colossal numbers.

Neutrinos were produced during the Big Bang, and experts calculate that there are approximately 55 million neutrinos per cubic meter of space. If any one of the three types of neutrinos happens to weigh a hundredth of a millionth as much as a proton, then it's quite possible that the neutrinos *are* the dark matter.[44] On the other hand, these same experts point out that current data indicate that neutrinos are too light to serve as dark matter.[45] Basically, while the neutrinos' masses added together may weigh as much as all ordinary, visible matter, the sum still equals only one-tenth of all matter, including dark matter. So the debate rages on about what constitutes dark matter.

About twenty years ago, physicists thought that neutrinos had no mass whatsoever. It was when scientists began postulat-

44. Brian Greene, *The Fabric of the Cosmos*, op. cit., p. 433.
45. Ibid.

ing that neutrinos had some light mass that they began to think of neutrinos as possible dark matter.

In the late 1980s, physicists changed course, thinking that neutrinos could not be dark matter. If neutrinos move near the speed of light, that means they are "hot" particles, and hot dark matter probably isn't the key to explaining the Big Bang and the creation of galaxies. It requires a lot of time for hot dark matter to create large-scale clusters of galaxies—more time than can be accounted for by the current age of the universe.

If dark matter doesn't consist of neutrinos, what is it? We're stuck with the same problem.

In the early 1980s, cosmologist J. Richard Bond coined the term "cold dark matter," which refers to particles that are heavier than neutrinos and that move slowly, hence might have formed the clusters of galaxies. Included among the cold dark matter candidates are the axions (named after a common detergent), photinos, zinos, and higgsinos. These are collectively known as super particles. Axions, for example, are very light, neutral particles that interact with tiny forces.

Physicists often talk about supersymmetry, in which every particle has a super partner with a different spin. For example, electrons and neutrinos, which are types of leptons, have a spin of one-half. The super partners of leptons are called sleptons, and their spins are zero. Quarks have super partners called squarks with spins of zero. Gluons, which hold the quarks together, have super partners called gluinos. A spin one photon that causes light has a super partner called a photino.

Of course, there's no evidence that any of these super particles exist. Nobody has ever seen one in the laboratory.

It's true that computer simulations have shown that cold dark matter could have created huge clusters of galaxies. But on the other hand, smaller galactic entities don't work with cold dark matter math. The simulations show that a thousand small satellite galaxies should surround the Milky Way, when in reality only ten satellite galaxies are around the Milky Way.[46]

While WIMPs remain popular choices for dark matter, many physicists believe that these particles don't interact enough to have helped much during the Big Bang. Some scientists speculate that there must be something out there that we haven't considered yet. Possibly the particles we seek are like neutrinos with heavier mass. These particles would be warm dark matter, a cross between the speeding, ultra-light hot dark matter neutrino and the slow-moving, heavier cold dark matter WIMPs.

The proposals for forms other than hot dark matter and cold dark matter are numerous. They include theories about strongly self-interacting dark matter, warm dark matter, repulsive dark matter, fuzzy dark matter, self-annihilating dark matter, and decaying dark matter.

Another theory of dark matter is that it consists of hydrogen gas. Much of the visible, ordinary matter in the universe is made of hydrogen. In fact, guesses put the amount of hydrogen in the universe at seventy-five percent of visible matter. Some people theorize that the dark matter is made up of small clouds of hydrogen gas. However, this seems unlikely because—you can probably guess the answer by now—we can observe hydrogen gas using radio, optical, ultraviolet, infrared, and X-ray telescopes.

Another notion about dark matter that is central to *His Dark Materials* is that dark matter equates to consciousness. In *His Dark Materials*, the Dust or dark matter knows what's happening everywhere at all times. It's an omniscient entity. It can make people aware of the future and past using dreams and other methods, such as the I Ching, Lyra's alethiometer, or Dr. Mary Malone's computer.

Some physicists claim that only a conscious entity, such as a

46. Tom Siegfried, *Strange Matters*, op. cit., p. 105.

human, can make measurements; and because the existence of matter depends on measurement, then it follows that the existence of the universe depends on consciousness.[47]

Of course, most physicists argue that measurement can occur without a conscious being taking the measurement. For example, a camera can measure distance and lighting, and it is not a conscious being.

In today's world, faith in spiritual aspects of life takes a backseat for most people to scientific materialism. While we enjoy the benefits of science, we're too busy to pause and consider deeply what it means to be human. In *His Dark Materials*, Pullman seems to be attacking traditional notions of God and religion, while supporting the notion of cosmic consciousness.

Dr. Amit Goswami, professor of physics at the Institute of Theoretical Sciences at the University of Oregon, has been promoting the idea (as has Pullman) that our cosmic, collective consciousness is the backbone of reality, far more so than matter itself. Dr. Goswami reports that he has spoken to numerous authorities in various scientific disciplines about his theories.

For example, physicist Murray Gell-Mann told Goswami that his generation of physicists had been brainwashed into thinking that all the fundamental aspects of quantum physics were discovered sixty years ago.[48] It was his feeling, apparently, that we have far more to discover about quantum physics than we think.

Cognitive psychologist Ulric Neisser told Dr. Goswami that his field isn't ready for consciousness yet. And according to Dr. Goswami, neurophysiologist Roger Sperry, physical chemist Ilya

47. Michio Kaku and Jennifer Thompson, *Beyond Einstein: The Cosmic Quest for the Theory of the Universe*. New York: Anchor Books, 1995, p. 48.
48. Amit Goswami, Richard E. Reed, and Maggie Goswami, *The Self-Aware Universe: How Consciousness Creates the Material World*. New York: Penguin Putnam, 1993, p. 4.

Prigogine, and physicist Carl Sagan all believed that everything is made of matter, there is nothing else to consider, and consciousness is a phenomenon of our brains. Finally, philosopher Karl Popper holds the view, according to Dr. Goswami, that consciousness must be separate from the brain in order to affect it.[49]

Clearly, most scientists believe in physics and scientific materialism as we know it today. However, a few believe that consciousness is more important in the universe than matter. They point to the fact that we must observe quantum objects to give them validity. They also point out that quantum objects, through wave properties, can be in more than one place at once and that they can influence other quantum objects that are far away. Hence, they argue, it is our observations that give these quantum objects value, and it is our consciousness that enables us to make the observations. More about this in a minute.

For now, let's trace the origins of scientific materialism and the roots of Philip Pullman's *His Dark Materials*.

In the seventeenth century, French mathematician and philosopher René Descartes visited the palace in Versailles. Here, he was enthralled by the "automata" in the palace gardens. These automata controlled the flow of water, the music, and even a giant Neptune, which rose from a pool in the gardens. Descartes began thinking that the world is an automaton, a machine, just like the palace garden.

Later, Descartes proposed his now-famous theory of dualism, which divided the world into two realms: the domain of science and matter (materialism) and the domain of the mind and religion. Descartes separated science from the powerful Church. This seems to be a main theme in *His Dark Materials*: separation of science from the powerful Church. The difference is that *His Dark Materials* puts forth the idea that our minds are intimately

49. Ibid., pp. 6–7.

connected to science (or dark matter and cosmic consciousness) itself.

In the mid 1600s, Isaac Newton contributed physics theories that established Descartes's "world as machine" ideas as scientific truth. Newton suggested the principle of *causal determinism*: given the laws of motion and the facts about where objects are before they move and how fast they're moving, we can predict the exact locations of the objects.

Going into the nineteenth century, classical physics thus had two main principles: the separation of science from the mind (often called *strong objectivity*) and causal determinism. Along came Albert Einstein. He added the famous theory of relativity, which among other things, suggested that the highest velocity in the universe is the speed of light, which is 300,000 kilometers (or 186,000 miles) per second. Einstein's theory further suggested that all interactions between objects in spacetime must be local: Objects travel one bit at a time with a finite velocity. This idea is often called *locality*.

As scientists explored the dualism, or separation of science and matter from the mind, they started to revise their thinking and came up with the notion of *material monism*. This means that everything in the universe, including our minds and consciousness, are composed of matter. Energy and force fields are intimately connected to matter, so they're included in this general notion of matter as well.

Because nobody knows how to prove the connections between mind, consciousness, and matter, scientists use the term *epiphenomenalism* to describe the derivation of consciousness from matter. In general terms, epiphenomenalism hypothesizes that consciousness is a series of properties of the brain, which is composed of matter.

In summary, proponents of *material realism* believe in five principles:

1. Causal determinism
2. Strong objectivity
3. Locality
4. Material monism
5. Epiphenomenalism

The closest *His Dark Materials* comes to supporting material realism is the argument that mind and matter are intertwined in some way (*epiphenomenalism* and *material monism*). I don't see evidence of *causal determinism* in the books, that we can predict the exact locations of objects. Nor do I see evidence of the separation of science from the mind, or *strong objectivity*. As for *locality*—all interactions between objects are local, and all objects travel one bit at a time with a finite velocity—this doesn't seem to ring true in *His Dark Materials*, either. People enter and exit from billions of parallel worlds simply by stepping through rips in spacetime, windows, or by flying through these constructs in the case of witches and angels. In addition, mental telepathy is common, which means objects (people, angels, other beings, brains) are interacting across far, as opposed to local, distances.

The opposite of material realism, which we've just described, is called *monistic idealism*. In this view, we have a universal or cosmic consciousness, which seems to be more in line with the philosophies of *His Dark Materials*.

An example of monistic idealism might be Buddhism, in which Nirmanakaya is the material realm and Samghogakaya is the mind and spirit realm. Both are united under Dharmakaya, the light of one consciousness. Other examples of a cosmic consciousness might be the atman of the Hindus and the Christian Holy Spirit.

Note the focus on consciousness rather than matter. Monistic idealism holds that everyone is united under one cosmic consciousness. If we think back to the discussions in this chapter about Dust and dark matter, it seems quite likely that *His Dark Materials* is tied more to monistic idealism than material realism. If the Dust and dark matter form our consciousness, then monistic idealism might be the underpinning of *His Dark Materials*.

When it comes to dark matter, about the only area of agreement among scientists is that it exists and that we think it consists primarily of elementary particles, as referenced in *His Dark Materials*. Today's scientists are working to identify these particles of dark matter, just as Lord Asriel and Dr. Mary Malone are working to identify them in *His Dark Materials*.

But there's something else in the universe that is closely related to dark matter, and this is called dark energy.

Part 3. Dark Energy

Recall from our earlier discussion that only 5 percent of the universe's mass is visible, ordinary matter, 25 percent is dark matter, and 70 percent is dark energy. While the numbers fluctuate depending on who's supplying them, scientists agree that the proportions are close. So while one scientist may claim that 70 percent of the universe is dark energy, another might claim that number to be 73 percent. Close enough for our purposes.

If you cut a hole or rip the fabric of the universe, as Will does with the subtle knife and as Lord Asriel does during his experiments in the far North, it's possible that you're tearing into the glue that binds the universe together. This may be why the worlds experience such tremors and anomalies in *The Amber Spyglass*. This may be why Will and Lyra absolutely must seal all the windows among the worlds, all the rips in spacetime, in the universe—although it does seem odd that simply by patching up holes, the entire universe can be spared collapse.

Dark energy may explain why the universe is expanding rather than shrinking. Dark energy might repel cosmic structures—think of it as pushing against the stars, planets, and so forth—with sufficient force to exceed the gravitational attraction of these structures. Hence, while the stars, planets, etc., are pushing toward each other, with the universe shrinking upon itself, it is the dark energy that overcomes this gravitational force and keeps the universe from collapsing.

Nobody really knows what dark energy is; it's at least as mysterious as dark matter.

As recently as the 1990s, cosmologists were still seeking answers about the expansion of the universe *without* assuming the existence of dark energy. Theories about cold microwave cosmic radiation came into play, which deals with how the earliest, smallest seeds of matter were laid out during the creation of the universe. Scientists used telescopes, satellites, and other equipment to measure the radiation temperature at different points in the sky. These points were separated by different angles. Oddly enough, by 2001, experiments on these temperatures, points, and angles confirmed that the universe is extremely close to flat.

Now, most of us think that the universe is some infinite void filled with planets, stars, cosmic dust, and other objects, and that the universe stretches forever in all directions. We hardly think that the universe is flat.

But current science tells us otherwise, and current science explains the flatness by conjecturing the existence of some sort of dark energy.

One theory about dark energy is that it is the vacuum energy proposed by Albert Einstein's cosmological constant. A fairly constant amount of this vacuum energy is in space, and as space stretches outward in its flat way, hence creating more space, we get more of this vacuum energy to fill in the void. The density of the vacuum energy remains the same—or constant—at all times.

As the universe expands, and as the density of vacuum energy remains stable, the density of matter in the universe decreases. Why? Suppose you have five grains of sand in a box that's one inch by one inch by one inch in dimension. Those five grains of sand have a specific density in that small box, right? Now you take the sand and put it in a much larger box, say one that is one foot by one foot by one foot in dimension. At this point, the same five grains of sand have a much smaller density in their newly expanded box.

When the universe was born, the vacuum energy was probably pretty small. If the vacuum energy density had been greater than the density of all the mass in the universe back then, the universe would have blown apart. There would have been no matter left to form the stars and planets. Today, however, experiments show that the vacuum energy density exceeds the visible matter density in the universe. This is why the universe is expanding.

Another theory about dark energy is that it is quintessence, a mysterious invisible fluid, a force field akin to Aristotle's fifth essence (hence the term, quint, or five, essence). Ancient physicists in Aristotle's time believed that everything was created from four elements: earth, water, fire, and air. The fifth essence or element was an all-pervasive component that caused the motion of the planets and moon. Today's physicists often divide everything into four areas, as well: ordinary, visible matter, radiation, neutrinos, and dark matter. And then there's the dark energy, which is an unknown realm. Today's fifth essence or element influences the evolution of the universe.

Quintessence supposedly exerts the type of force that pushes things in on themselves, a sort of negative pressure against the structures of the universe. It's similar to Einstein's vacuum space cosmological constant, but a key difference is that quintessence isn't a constant—it isn't uniform. Because its force changes throughout space, it can exert more force in some areas of space and time, and it can be weaker elsewhere.

How can quintessence be dark energy that changes in force depending on location and time in space? Scientists postulate that quintessence is a scalar field. In the case of physics, a field sits in space but is part of space itself; and it affects other structures and values in space. For example, a particle of matter is really a knot or twist in space, and it is in a quantum field.

Setting aside quantum fields, which are extremely complex, physics defines other types of fields. There are scalar fields, which have to do with quintessence, as well as vector and tensor fields.

At any point in space, a vector field has a strength value and a direction. An electromagnetic field is an example of a vector field; it has strength and direction at every point in space. Think about how a compass works. If you're pointing north, the compass needle moves north, aligning itself with Earth's magnetic field.

A tensor field, such as gravity, is a bit more complex. Many factors determine how strong gravity is at any one point.

As for scalar fields, they have strength but no direction. They can exert more force, or be "thicker," at one place or time than at other places or times. The energy in a quintessence field can, therefore, differ from place to place, from time to time.

Dark energy might be the force in *His Dark Materials* that causes tears in the fabric of spacetime, causing near collapse of the billions of parallel worlds. As we've noted, as the universe expands the amount of dark energy increases. Billions of years from now, it's possible that the dark energy will be so strong that it will pull space apart, stretch space so quickly and with such force that galaxy clusters break apart, followed by the disintegration of individual galaxies, such as the Milky Way. In fact, too much dark energy may someday shred all matter into a rapidly expanding realm of outer space.

But this is all conjecture. The bottom line remains: We don't know what dark energy is, any more than we really know what makes up the dark matter.

ANGELS, G⊕D, AND PARADISE

3

Angels play important roles in the Jewish and Christian Bibles, and as we'll soon see, in many other religions as well. As early as Genesis (16:7–11), God's angel meets Hagar and tells her to return to Sarai to have a child, who will be Ishmael. Soon after in Genesis, two angels save Lot and his family from death in Sodom. Then an angel intervenes and saves Isaac from Abraham's knife.

It goes on and on. References to angels are abundant in the Bible. In the New Testament, Matthew (1:20–24), an angel appears to Joseph while he's dreaming and tells Joseph about Mary's conception by the Holy Spirit. Later, we're told that at the end of time, angels will separate the wicked from the just.

This book, as you may have gathered by now, is not a religious text. Rather, I'm exploring many of the subjects I find fascinating in *His Dark Materials*. First, I covered Dust and dark matter because these subjects are the core to all else in Philip Pullman's trilogy. And while I considered writing next about parallel worlds, which also are key components to the trilogy, I decided to break up the scientific topics with the lighter ones. Not that the subjects of Angels, God, and Heaven are light. But they don't require deep discourse about physics and unknown entities throughout the galaxies.

So while this chapter focuses on traditionally religious ideas, it's not my intention, as author, to support specific religious ideas over others. It's not my position to suggest that angels, God, or heaven exist—or that they don't: I leave such contemplations to my readers.

With that in mind, let's return to the subjects at hand. First up: What roles do angels play in *His Dark Materials*? How are angels depicted in the three books?

In *The Subtle Knife*, the old servant Thorgold tells Lyra that the Church teaches that angels are pure spirit. He says that, before the world was created, the angels rebelled and were ejected from heaven and sent to hell (*The Subtle Knife*, page 47). This sounds very familiar, doesn't it? It's very similar to what we learn in the Judeo-Christian religions. And *His Dark Materials* is clearly based on Christian, albeit Catholic, theology.

Later in *The Subtle Knife*, we learn that angels come from other worlds and pass through the world containing Cittagàzze. A child named Joachim Lorenz tells the witch Serafina that the angels call themselves *bene elim*. Sometimes, he says, the angels are called the *Watchers*. Angels are spirits, who carry messages from heaven. They shine like fireflies, they have wings, and in ancient times, they had children with humans (*The Subtle Knife*, page 137). Later, we learn that they shine like sunlight, they look like tall, naked, winged humans; some are male, others are female. Most interesting, they are distinct individuals who share a "shimmering, darting play of intelligence" (*The Subtle Knife*, page 140). The angels are ancient beings, and their awareness spreads to "the remotest corners of the universe." To the witch Ruta Skadi, the angels are like huge structures of architecture that are everywhere, possessed of vast intelligence and feelings; they are immortal (*The Subtle Knife*, page 141).

It seems that the angels in *His Dark Materials* are omniscient Watcher spirit-creatures. While they are composed entirely of spirit, at least up to this point in our reading of the trilogy, they also manage to produce children with humans. They've lived forever in both male and female form.

Things become even more interesting as we continue reading. When Dr. Mary Malone uses her computer to communicate with shadow particles, the Dust tells her that Dust equals dark matter, which equals the shadow particles, which in turn, equals consciousness; and if those links weren't enough to comprehend at once, the Dust aka dark matter aka shadow particles aka consciousness also equals the billions of angels. The angels are structures made of Dust. Because the matter and spirit are one, we assume that this is how spirit-creatures are able to bear children. Dr. Malone also learns that Dust "intervened" in human evolution (*The Subtle Knife*, page 248).

At this point, then, we deduce that there are billions of angels, and while they are indeed omniscient Watcher spirit-creatures, they are composed of Dust, which is dark matter. They've lived forever in both male and female form, they helped during human evolution, and they are capable of having children with humans.

Later in *The Amber Spyglass*, two angels appear to Will, and they tell him that, because angels don't have flesh, they are weaker than humans. Balthamos and Baruch, the two angels, are not of a "high order" of angels, they say (*The Amber Spyglass*, page 11). Soon after, we learn that dead people sometimes become angels, and that indeed, Baruch was a human man four thousand years ago. We also learn that angels can read each other's minds from long distances; that is, they have mental telepathy (*The Amber Spyglass*, page 22). Another bit of information to add to our knowledge about angels in *His Dark Materials* is that Balthamos is a shapeshifter: he can change form, though he says it's humiliating for him to change from an angel into any other form (*The Amber Spyglass*, page 23).

Metatron is an extremely powerful and strong angel in *The Amber Spyglass*. The Authority reigns in the Kingdom with Metatron as his Regent. Baruch tells Will that most of the angels are against the Authority and Metatron. Balthamos adds that the Authority calls himself by various names: "God, the Creator, the Lord, Yahweh, El, Adonai, the King, the Father, the Almighty." Yet the Authority was not a Creator. Rather, the Authority was the first angel made from Dust. He lied to subsequent angels, telling them that he had created them. But all angels came from Dust, not from the Authority (*The Amber Spyglass*, pages 28–32). Metatron has ruled for four thousand years. He was once called Enoch, the son of Jared, the son of Mahalel (*The Amber Spyglass*, page 63).

Before we continue with notions of God, the Authority, and heaven, as depicted in *His Dark Materials*, let's summarize what we know about angels in the trilogy. Then we'll explore angels, as we think we know them today.

In *His Dark Materials*, billions of angels are omniscient Watcher spirit-creatures, and they are composed of Dust, which is dark matter. They've lived forever in both male and female forms, they helped during human evolution, and they are capable of having children with humans. They are weaker than humans, and they are ranked in some sort of hierarchy. Although dead people can turn into angels, most angels were never human. Angels are shapeshifters and have mental telepathy. The Authority was the first angel made from Dust, and four thousand years ago, he gave the title of Regent, or ruler of the entire universe, to the powerful angel Metatron. Now let's see how closely *His Dark*

Materials follows the notions we've believed of angels here on Earth.

In addition to the Old and New Testaments, angels are found in the Book of Mormon, the Koran, and the Dead Sea Scrolls. And many religions incorporate angels into their theology. Let's trace the origins of angels:

In the ancient period between A.D. 1–500, the Roman world was one of pagan polytheism and emperor worship. Early Christians, following the examples set by the Romans and others, often worshipped angels, Michael being especially popular. People thought that angels were perfect beings created by God and that their bodies were made of light.

During the second century, the Gnostics believed in two gods, one good, the other evil. In addition, spirit was good, and matter was not. From the good god, the spiritual one, emanated a vast number of angels.

In approximately A.D. 500, a Syrian mystic known as Dionysius the Areopagite wrote *Celestial Hierarchy*. Dionysius proclaimed that he was the convert "Dionysius the Areopagite," a member of the Athenian council of elders, to whom Paul refers in Acts 17:34. Many people called him the Pseudo-Dionysius because of his pretentious claim.

Pseudo-Dionysius had a huge impact on the church, though he was viewed largely as a fraud. Basically, he divided the angels into three classes. The first class consisted of Seraphim, Cherubim, and Thrones; these angels were closest to God. The second consisted of Dominations, Principalities, and Powers; and these angels were enlightened by the first class of angels. The third consisted of Virtues, Archangels, and other Angels; and these lowest-ranking angels were enlightened by the second class.

Throughout the ages, other sources and authorities have ranked angels into celestial hierarchies, as well. For example, Moses Maimonides in the *Mishne Torah* ranks them as follows:

1. Chaioth ha-Qadesh
2. Auphanim
3. Aralim
4. Chashmalim
5. Seraphim
6. Malachim
7. Elohim
8. Bene Elohim
9. Kerubim
10. Ishim

Notice the type of angel in the number eight position. In *His Dark Materials*, Joachim Lorenz tells Serafina that the angels he knows about call themselves *bene elim*. The term *bene elohim* literally translates into the phrase, sons of God.

St. Ambrose, St. Jerome, and St. Gregory the Great all listed the angels in orders very similar to Pseudo-Dionysius. There are a few differences, such as the elimination of Principalities and Virtues from St. Jerome's list.

The Old Testament introduces the orders of Seraphim and Cherubim, and the New Testament introduces the orders of Archangels and Angels. The Judeo-Christian Bibles firmly establish the existence of nine types of angels.

Metatron, who has more than one hundred other names, is known in the Bible as the lesser God. According to Gustav Davidson in the excellent resource *A Dictionary of Angels*,[50] Metatron is "perhaps the greatest of all the heavenly hierarchs, the first (as also the last) of the ten Archangels. . . ." Philip Pullman calls Metatron the Regent of God. In our real world, Metatron is known as the king of angels, chancellor of Heaven, chief

50. Gustav Davidson, *A Dictionary of Angels, including the Fallen Angels*. New York: The Free Press/Macmillan, Inc., 1967, p. 192.

of the ministering angels, and the lesser God, among other titles. His job is to sustain all of humanity (a daunting task, at best—I suggest he needs more help!). Metatron states in *His Dark Materials* that he is Enoch, and in reality, he is thought to be the patriarch Enoch, who claims to be the mighty angel, Michael.

Metatron has been described as the "dark angel who wrestled with Jacob at Penial (Genesis 32) and . . . it is said that Exodus 23:20 refers to Metatron: "Behold, I send an angel before thee, to keep thee in the way and to bring thee unto the place where I have been prepared" (usually applied to John the Baptist) and Exodus 23:22: "My name is him."[51]

Baruch of *His Dark Materials* might be based on the angel Barach, who is referenced in the Bible. Or he may be based simply on the Hebrew word Baruch, which means Blessed.

Lord Asriel, of course, might be based on Ashriel, also known as Azrael and Azriel. Ashriel is one of the "seven angels with dominion over the Earth. He is the angel who separates the soul from the body at death."[52]

In the first angelic hierarchy, we have the Seraphim, Cherubim, and Thrones. The Seraphim each have six pairs of wings: "In the year that king Ozias died, I saw the Lord sitting upon a throne, high and elevated: and his train filled the temple. Upon it stood the Seraphims: the one had six wings, and the other had six wings . . ." (Isaiah 6:1–3). The word *seraphim* means "having a fiery love." It also means "carrier of warmth" and implies the power to purify men using intense love. It does not appear that the Seraphim play central roles in *His Dark Materials*.

Nor do the Cherubim, which represent light and the knowledge of good things. The name Cherubim means "the power to

51. Ibid.
52. Ibid., pp. 56–57. Also see the entry for Azrael in *The Columbia Encyclopedia*, Sixth Edition, 2001, as found at: http://www.bartleby.com/65/az/Azrael.html.

know and see God." The Cherubim first appear in Genesis: "And he cast out Adam; and placed before the paradise of pleasure Cherubims, and a flaming sword, turning every way, to keep the way of the tree of life" (Genesis 3:24). In Exodus, the instructions for building the Ark of the Covenant include the making and placement of golden Cherubims: "Thou shalt also make two Cherubims of beaten gold, on the two sides of the oracle. Let one Cherub be on the one side, and the other on the other. Let them cover both sides of the propitiary, spreading their wings, and covering the oracle . . ." (Exodus 25:18–20).

The Thrones communicate God's will to lesser angels. They are patrons of peace.

The second angelic hierarchy consists of Dominations, Principalities, and Powers. Lower in the angelic hierarchy than Thrones, the Dominations also communicate God's will to lesser angels. The Principalities perform executive duties related to how angels interact with humans. The Powers have unshakable courage and fight Satanic evil.

The third angelic hierarchy consists of Virtues, Archangels, and other Angels. It is somewhere within this ranking that we expect to find Baruch and Balthamos, who say that they are angels of low-ranking order. This third angelic hierarchy cares for humans and their provinces. The Virtues, who are extremely strong, enforce the Dominations' orders. The Archangels watch over people, empires, provinces, and even tiny villages. There may be an Archangel protecting the village where I live, and a different Archangel protecting the city where you live.

Finally, we have the Angels. They are the lowest order in the hierarchy and appear throughout both the Old and New Testaments. They include the Guardian Angels. I believe that Baruch and Balthamos are both Angels—possibly, they are Guardian Angels.

There is a final type of angel, called the Angel of the Lord. Supposedly, God created all angels except for one, the Angel of the Lord. We'll talk about this angel a bit later in the chapter, when we navigate through the even more complex subject of God.

For now, let's trace the history of angels throughout time and see what people think about them today.

During the Middle Ages, between 500 and 1500, people thought that angels were created when God created the material world. Thomas Aquinas believed that angels possessed limited knowledge, bestowed upon them by God, and that they didn't have the ability to learn more. Guardian angels, those who are Watchers over each human, were a popular idea during the Middle Ages.

Thomas Aquinas was one of the most influential people in Christianity. In his *Summa Theologiae*, he asked 118 questions about angels. He attempted to answer many of those questions. In addition, he wrote eight proofs that showed why angels exist. He said that angels are aeviternal, which means their basic natures don't change, but they can change their actions. So while they don't get sick or die, they can travel across the universe. In contrast, humans are temporal, meaning our basic natures can change (we get sick and die, for example), as well as our actions (while we may not travel across the universe, we do travel to far-away places). And finally, Aquinas said that God is eternal, meaning that he exists forever, totally beyond concepts such as change and time.

Between 1500 and 1648, during the Reformation period, the kindness of angels was stressed. While many people believed in guardian angels, many did not. Article twelve of the Belgic Confession in 1561 stated that God created "the angels good, to be his messengers and to serve his elect," and went on to describe fallen angels, everlasting perdition, devils, evil spirits, and eternal damnation.[53] The main thrust of the church during this period

---

53. "The Belgic Confession of Faith," *Reformed Confessions of the 16th Century*, A.C. Coleridge, editor. Philadelphia: Westminster, 1966, p. 196.

seemed to be on Satan, devils, and demons. Dante's *Divine Comedy* focused strongly on Satan, hell, purgatory, and demons.

John Calvin and John Milton both contributed a lot about angels during this period. Calvin kept to the Bible and avoided ranking angels into hierarchies. Nor did he take sides in the debate about guardian angels. Calvin did believe that a huge body of angels were Watchers over man. John Milton's *Paradise Lost* was a major influence on Philip Pullman while conceiving and writing *His Dark Materials*.

Milton was blind when he wrote *Paradise Lost* in 1667. In the masterpiece, he presented two perfect worlds, one being the heaven of God, and the other being the paradise of the newly created human couple. Heaven, which sparkled and was full of delight, was the place where angels worshipped God. There was nothing human in Milton's heaven, although God's heaven did provide the source for all earthly existence. Separated from this perfect heaven by "worlds and worlds" and a "vast Ethereal Sky" was the domain of Adam and Eve, the earthbound paradise of the newly created human couple. Most notable in terms of *His Dark Materials*, Milton's Adam and Eve discover sexual maturity, and this is a key ingredient to the way life was before the Fall. The Christian heaven, paradise regained, might therefore include the joys of physical love.

In *His Dark Materials*, Will is Adam and Lyra is Eve. When they fall in love in *The Amber Spyglass*, the worlds change forever. Philip Pullman tells readers that growing up is okay, it's not a sin to fall in love, and indeed, it's perhaps love itself that the world needs.

From 1648 on, rationalism took over and many people started questioning whether the Bible was indeed the word of God. Along with this more "enlightened" thinking about the Bible, people began rejecting the idea that angels exist. Angels became representations of holiness, goodness, and kindness rather than actual beings.

Emanuel Swedenborg, who lived between 1688 and 1772, claimed that angels guided him while he wrote thirty books. A vision sent by God enabled Swedenborg to talk to angels, he claimed. He wasn't particularly popular with orthodox Christians during his time, but he did contribute much lore about mysticism and angels. For example, he wrote that angels eat food, read books, get married, have sex, and breathe air. Many of his theories, as we'll see in a moment, are still believed by people today.

Karl Barth, who lived between 1886 and 1968, taught that angels do not communicate with humans. Their sole communication is with God, and they serve only to dispense messages from God. How angels dispense messages without communicating with the recipients of those messages is unclear.

Geddes MacGregor, a now-retired distinguished professor of philosophy at the University of Southern California, believes that angels are extraterrestrial beings.[54]

During the past few decades, belief in angels and other spiritual entities has increased. New Age ideas have captured the minds of many, and with New Age comes studies of astrology, witchcraft, and the occult. With darker studies on the rise, biblical contemplations are also increasing: You can easily find books about demons, Satan, and angels.

I have a few modern books about angels. I've never practiced New Age religions, but during a period of personal sadness, I obtained angel books in an effort to find comfort. Did it work? Yes, and I also found comfort in angel oracles and even fairy oracles. I'm not suggesting that you immediately turn to oracles to turn

54. Geddes MacGregor, *Angels: Ministers of Grace*. St. Paul, MN: Paragon House Publishers, 1991.

your life around or help lift your spirits during dark times. But I do recognize, from personal experience, that people who believe in spiritual entities, including angels, can find solace and warmth. During troubled times, people need relief. During the past decade alone, people have seen a dramatic rise in poverty, war, terrorism, natural disasters, divorce, and hatred simply for the sake of hating. Crime frightens us all, and the general society is riddled with prejudice, unemployment, poor education, and far too much misery. Times are tough. Surveys of Americans indicate that one-third of the population believes in angels.[55]

Peter Kreeft is a professor of philosophy at Boston College. He teaches a class about angels. His book, *Angels (and Demons)*, attempts to explain what angels really are and what they do with their time. Kreeft believes that angelology is a science, that it uses the scientific method of gathering and explaining data.[56] Contrary to *His Dark Materials*, Kreeft writes that everything in the universe consists of matter except angels. He says that angels cannot die or be destroyed, that they are pure spirit, and that they are not light. They are visitors who don't belong in this universe.[57] Further, humans cannot become angels upon death,[58] which is another point that contradicts the nature of angels in *His Dark Materials*.

It is generally believed by many people that angels communicate with one another through some form of mental telepathy. In addition, most people who believe in angels think that angels

55. Matthew Fox, Ph.D., an Episcopal priest, and Rupert Sheldrake, Ph.D., a biologist, in *The Physics of Angels: Exploring the Realm Where Science and Spirit Meet*. San Francisco: HarperSanFrancisco, 1996, p. 1.
56. Peter Kreeft, *Angels (and Demons): What Do We Really Know About Them?* San Francisco: Ignatius Press, 1995, p. 7.
57. Ibid., p. 47.
58. Ibid., p. 54.

travel instantaneously, that they can be anywhere at any given time. Most people believe that angels have no gender; that is, they aren't female or male. Most people believe that angels cannot have sex with humans. Note that in *His Dark Materials*, angels do have gender and they are capable of having children with humans.

Some people do link angels to dark matter. They point out that matter is "now more like a process than a thing" and that "90 to 99 percent of the matter in the cosmos is dark matter, utterly unknown to us. It is as if physics has discovered the cosmic unconscious."[59] In fact, it is believed by some that even the sun is a conscious entity, and for proof, we need only look at the fact that our own mental activity "is associated with complex electromagnetic patterns in our brains." Because the sun is highly sensitive to electromagnetism, then it's possible for the sun itself to think, to dream, and to be full of cosmic consciousness.[60] Indeed, if the sun is conscious, then all the other stars might be conscious as well. And the stars might hold the angels within them; in fact, the intelligence of the stars might be the angels themselves.[61]

There's one final thing we must discuss: the Angel of the Lord. According to some interpretations of the Bible, God created all angels except one, which happened to be his own angel: the Angel of the Lord. While he's clearly called the Angel of the Lord (Genesis 16:7), he's also known as "My presence" (Exodus 33:14), "Captain of the host of the Lord" (Joshua 5:14), and "messenger of the covenant" (Mal. 3:1). Some people think that this Angel of the Lord is simply another, special angel that God sends to help mankind rather than an angel that God did not cre-

59. Matthew Fox and Rupert Sheldrake, op.cit., p. 9.
60. Ibid., pp. 18–19.
61. Ibid., p. 20.

ate. I am in no position to answer this question for you, but I do note that in *His Dark Materials*, God is an angel Himself.

In fact, in *His Dark Materials*, God is the first angel. God is not the Creator, as religious people believe on Earth today. Instead, as Baruch tells Will (*The Amber Spyglass*, pages 30–32), the Authority (or God) was never the Creator, but simply the first angel formed of Dust (or dark matter), who then created all the other angels.

Later, Baruch tells Lord Asriel that the Authority is in a crystal chamber inside the Clouded Mountain (*The Amber Spyglass*, page 60). We also learn that the angels have been rebelling against God, the Authority, since he created them. At this point, a huge rebellion is occurring that includes angels, humans, and beings from all worlds. The Kingdom of Heaven will be removed, and all beings will live in a free Republic of Heaven (*The Amber Spyglass*, pages 210–11).

Finally, toward the end of *His Dark Materials*, Lyra and Will see the Authority in his crystal litter. The crystal prison is smeared with blood from the food of cliff ghasts. It's just hanging among some rocks. God, the Authority, is a pathetic wretch, entombed for thousands of years within the crystal prison. He's cowering, terrified; he's near-blind, he's weeping. He can't wait to die. Lyra and Will gently lift him from the crystal, and because of his frailty, the air itself is sufficient to disperse what's left of him into the wind. He simply vanishes before their eyes (*The Amber Spyglass*, page 410).

Needless to say, the Authority is nothing like the God we know from the Old and New Testaments. In the industrialized Western, Judeo-Christian world from which Pullman extracts his theology for *His Dark Materials*, God is generally understood to be "All powerful, all knowing, and all good; who created out of nothing the universe and everything in it with the exception of Himself; who is uncreated and eternal, a noncorporeal spirit who created, loves, and can grant eternal life to humans."[62] In addition, God is usually considered male.

It's beyond the scope of this book to consider whether God is all good, loving all life, etc. Those subjects are better suited to theological texts. For now, it's enough to note that God is thought to be the creator, while the Authority is not the Creator. *His Dark Materials* suggests that while there indeed might *be* a Creator, it is not the Authority.

Modern thinkers ponder how we can have free will if there is an omniscient God. This is central to *His Dark Materials*, for the only way free will is created in the trilogy is by disposing of the Authority and all who serve him. If God knows everything—past, present, and future—and has total power, then how can we hold ourselves responsible for bad decisions? If our futures are not predetermined, does this imply that God's power is limited? And if so, how extensive are His limitations?

Yet despite questions that many of us ask, most humans worldwide believe in an omniscient spiritual being, someone much larger than Pullman's Authority.

For Hindus, God is omniscient, omnipotent, and not made of matter. The Hindus also worship other gods, but for the most part, these are perceived as manifestations of the supreme God. In the Baha'i religion, the prophet Bahaullah proclaimed that God is omniscient and all-perceiving. Islamic tradition gives Allah many names, such as Real Truth, the Omnipotent, the Hearer, and the Omniscient. The Buddhist Sakyamuni—a name for the Buddha—was omniscient. The Tantric faith says that we should aim for omniscience ourselves, by which we will perceive cosmic consciousness, an all-knowing understanding of the universe. The Persian religion of Zoroastrianism portrays the god Or-

---

62. Michael Shermer, *Why People Believe Weird Things: Pseudoscience, Superstition, and Other Confusions of Our Time.* New York: W.H. Freeman, 1998, p. 10.

mazd as omniscient. In Jainism, an Indian religion, monks become omniscient by meditating. Even the ancient sphinx with its lion's body and human head, was considered omniscient.

For as long as people have believed in an omniscient God, people have questioned his existence. In *His Dark Materials*, the Authority turns out to be ancient Dust, yet beings on billions of worlds believe he is the all-knowing, elusive, and mysterious Creator. In our own reality, people wonder about God's nature as well.

The German theologian Paul Tillich, who lived between 1886 and 1965, wrote:

"If you start with the question whether God does or does not exist, you can never reach Him; and if you assert that He does exist, you can reach Him even less than if you assert that He does not exist. A God whose existence or nonexistence you can argue is a thing beside others within the universe of existing things." In Tillich's view, scientists actually do religion a service when they attempt to refute it by showing that there is no evidence that God exists. This stance forces religious leaders to ponder the meaning of God in great depth. Further, says Tillich, "theologians who boldly assert that God exists because they have received His authoritative revelations are far more dangerous for religion. . . . Theologians who make of God a highest being who has given some people information about Himself, provoke inescapably the resistance of those who are told they must subject themselves to the authority of this information."[63]

Of course, Philip Pullman's trilogy is concerned with the God of the Christian Bible. But our world alone has seen many thousands of deities since the dawn of time. Imagine a universe of billions of worlds, with each world supporting five thousand gods and goddesses. Simple multiplication leads to the conclu-

63. Paul Tillich, *Theology of Culture*. New York: Oxford University Press, 1959, p. 4–5.

sion that, in *His Dark Materials*, beings on these billions of worlds might worship far more than the Authority.

Of course, we read with the assumption that all of these billions of worlds are closely aligned parallel worlds (see Chapter 6, "Parallel Worlds") with enormous similarities. Hence, if the Church rules in Lyra's world, it must rule in the other worlds as well. But logic tells us otherwise. If a slight mutation occurs between world one and world two, then another slight mutation ripples from world two to world three. By the time we get to world 500,000, the changes as we shift to world 500,001 could alter world 500,001 in such a way that it barely resembles world one at all. The millionth parallel world could have a totally different notion of God from the first world. Not to mention the billionth, or the ten billionth world.

Will's world is much like ours. So we know that there are worlds in *His Dark Materials* where beings have worshipped thousands of gods across the centuries. Even in the modern era, our planet Earth is not dominated by Christianity. We support a multitide of religions, stretching back thousands of years and probably spanning thousands of years into the future.

One wonders where these gods fit into the billions of worlds of the Authority and *His Dark Materials*. If Dust is the same as dark matter, which is the same as cosmic consciousness; and if Dust or dark matter formed the Authority and all of the angels, then where do the many thousands of gods fit into Pullman's universe? Are they also made of Dust? Are they part of the cosmic consciousness? If so, why do we never hear about or see them in the trilogy?

Primitive cultures on Earth assigned spiritual identities to a wide realm of nature. Shamans, or wise ones, which we discuss further in Chapter 11, generally were the ones who appeased the spirits, begged them for help, and communicated with them for the tribe. The spirits were generally all-knowing but invisible to all but the shaman. In addition, the spirits usually had human form and habits. They grew angry and sad, they walked and talked, they had sex. This was an animistic type of religion.

Over time, these animistic spirits evolved into more abstract deities. People began to think of their deities in terms of human events. For example, there were gods of blacksmiths, goddesses of childbirth, and so forth. And as they evolved further, these gods and goddesses assumed increasingly human dimensions. They wore certain outfits, they looked a certain way. They lived in pecking orders, or hierarchies, similar to human hierarchies. One was a leader, the others followed. They had specific duties to perform, and they often worked in groups.

Gods are separate from human beings, and they dwell primarily in heaven. In some religions, such as Buddhism, the gods originated as people, and only through prayer and spiritual purity, did they rise to the elevated plane of godhood. In some cultures, ancestors attain godhood, such as the Sumerian god Dumuzi or the Norse god Balder.[64]

According to Manfred Lurker, in his *Dictionary of Gods and Goddesses,* "A basic element in all religions is the awareness, both intellectual and emotional, of man's dependence on nonhuman powers: powers which we conceive as personal, and vis-à-vis which we normally stand in a reciprocal relationship. Gods and demons are the forms taken by these powers . . . in the shape of light and darkness, sun and moon, fire and water, bird and snake. The divine can reveal itself in all the phenomena of nature. . . ."[65]

Further, Lurker explains that the notions of gods and demons differ based on religion. In Hinduism and Buddhism, he writes, the deities rank approximately on the level of angels and saints.

---

64. Michael Jordan, *The Encyclopedia of Gods.* Facts on File, 1993, p. viii.
65. Manfred Lurker, *Dictionary of Gods and Goddesses.* Routledge Press, 1987, p. vii.

"There are mortal gods, gods who die (like Baldr and Osiris) and demonic beings whom death cannot touch (for example, the Devas.)"[66]

If the creation story of the Cheyenne people, to give one example, were incorporated into *His Dark Materials*, we'd get a very different set of novels. The Cheyenne believe that the Great Power created the world, and way up north was a paradise where it was always warm and food was abundant. Everyone—all animals and people—loved each other in paradise. The red people, according to the story, were closest to the Great Power; the white people were crafty and manipulative; and the hairy people lived in caves until they vanished. The Great Power taught the red people how to survive: to hunt, to make clothes. Later, the Great Medicine Man in the sky gave the people food, such as corn and buffalo.

The Chinese have a very different story about the creation of the world. In the beginning of all time, a huge cosmic egg contained chaos, which was a mixture of yin (female, passive, cold, dark, wet) and yang (male, active, hot, light, dry). Also within the yin-yang was Phan Ku, who broke out of the primal egg. Phan Ku separated chaos into all the opposites, such as light and darkness, sky and ground. For 18,000 years, Phan Ku separated the sky and the ground until heaven was 30,000 miles higher than the Earth. Phan Ku was a major giant: He had horns and tusks, and he was coated in hair. Using a gigantic chisel and equally large mallet, he created the oceans and mountains, and all other forms of landscape. He also made the moon, stars, and planets. Unlike the God of Judaism and Christianity, Phan Ku died, whereupon his skull rose and settled at the very top of the sky, his voice became thunder, his breath became wind. In fact, his legs and arms became the four directions of north, south, east, and west. If that

66. Ibid., p. viii.

were not enough, his blood became the waters, his flesh became the soil. And stories say that humans were derived from fleas in his hair.

A very well-known story of creation comes from Iceland and Scandinavia. The Norse people, or Vikings, recorded their beliefs in what is called the Younger Edda, written by Snorri Sturluson in approximately 1220. Sturluson based his Younger Edda on the oral (spoken) myths of the Elder or Poetic Edda. In this story, the world was created from the body of the Evil Ice Giant, Ymir.

As the story goes, King Gylfi, who ruled what we now call Sweden, learned about the Aesir, the gods from Valhalla. Gylfi disguised himself and went to Valhalla to meet the High One and learn all about the Aesir and the beginning of the world.

The High One explained that there were two atmospheres, one in the north, the other in the south. The northern atmosphere was dark and icy; the southern was light and warm. Between the two atmospheres was total emptiness, called Ginnungagap. Within the void of Ginnungagap, the cold northern air mingled with the warm southern air, creating moisture, and hence, life began to form. The first form of life was the Evil Ice Giant called Ymir.

Ymir was alone in Ginnungagap, but he lay down, and while resting, his armpits gave birth to a man and a woman, and his legs mated to create a son. A family of ogres was born. As the ice melted in Ginnungagap, it turned into a cow giant named Auohumla, whose milk turned into nutritious rivers. A man arose from some ice that Auohumla was licking, and he was Buri the Strong, whose son Bor married Bestla, a daughter of the original ogres. Bor and Bestla had a child, the great god Odin, as well as other children, the gods Vili and Ve. These gods rose up and killed Ymir, the Evil Ice Giant, and then took the giant's corpse to the middle of Ginnungagap, where they transformed his blood into the oceans and his body into the earth. Mountains formed from his bones; and rocks from his teeth. His brains became the clouds. As with the Chinese creation story, Ymir's skull became the top of the sky; but unlike the Chinese story, Ymir's skull was held up in the north, south, east, and west by four dwarves. Finally, the gods Odin, Vili, and Ve made a man and a woman out of a fallen ash tree and a fallen elm.

As a final example of the many thousands of deities other than the Authority, or Judeo-Christian God, we turn to the Hindu religion of India. Our sole purpose in drawing some of these other, radically different deity stories is to point out that in *His Dark Materials* there is no room for the other deities of the world. Where are the Norse gods? Where are the Hindu gods? The Chinese gods? The Indian gods? This is not necessarily a drawback of the fiction, which stands superbly on its own. Rather, as noted earlier, we wonder how these gods fit into Pullman's billions of worlds: Are they also made of Dust, are they part of the cosmic consciousness to which Lyra, Will, Mary Malone, and others are connected? What happens to the people of all other cultures in the universe of *His Dark Materials*?

The Hindu religion has a variety of gods, which are metaphors for "the single absolute principle eventually called Brahman, a principle that is everywhere and nowhere, everything and nothing."[67] The Father of all people is the male force of heaven, who reached down and mated with his daughter Earth. A god of fire called Agni created the hot fire needed to kindle the passion between heaven and Earth. Arising from this union were the Angirases, who mediated between gods and people.

Another Hindu myth is based on Purusa, a thousand-headed, thousand-footed man, who was so big he enveloped heaven, Earth, and the entire universe from the beginning to the end of time. Early gods sacrified Purusa, and his bottom became our

---

67. David Adams Leeming and Margaret Adams Leeming, *A Dictionary of Creation Myths*. New York: Oxford University Press, 1995, p. 139.

world. His mouth turned into "the wise Brahmin priest and the god Indra. His arms became the warrior caste, his thighs the common people, and his feet the lowest of the low. . . . From Purusa's mind came the moon, from his eye the sun, from his breath the wind . . ." and so forth.[68]

This is only a small sampling of Hindu creation theory. Other theories involve primal eggs, the waters creating everything, and other stories surrounding Purusa.

One common theme throughout many religions is the idea of heaven. Little is said about heaven in *His Dark Materials*. We're told that there's a Kingdom of heaven, that the "Kingdom of heaven has been known by that name since the Authority first set himself above the rest of the angels" (*The Amber Spyglass*, page 210). We're next told that "this world is different. We intend to be free citizens of the Republic of heaven" (*The Amber Spyglass*, page 211).

But we will save the discussion of heaven for Chapter 7, where we talk about other theories related to the afterlife: heaven, the harpies, and hell.

68. Ibid., p. 140.

WI+CHES

4

Witches play a central role in *His Dark Materials*. More than once, they save Lyra, Will, and their friends. But the witches in *His Dark Materials* aren't like the Halloween witches we've all heard about since childhood. They don't wear big black hats, cackle, and cast evil spells that cause your house to go *poof*. They don't have warts, and they're not ancient hags. Well, they *are* ancient, but somehow they've retained the beauty of youth.

The first hint we have that the witches in *His Dark Materials* are good is in *The Golden Compass*, when John Faa and his friends decide to ask the witches for help. They intend to go to Trollesund, Lapland's main port, where the witches maintain a consulate. John Faa tells his friends that to find and rescue their children, they need the help of the witches (*The Golden Compass*, page 163).

In addition, we learn that Farder Coram was once very close to a particular witch; in fact, he saved her life. He explains that the incident occurred forty years ago, but to witches, forty years is a relatively short amount of time. Witches live to extremely old ages. He also comments that witches and their daemons can remain far apart (*The Golden Compass*, page 164). For humans, of course, daemons must be kept very close.

Upon arriving in Trollesund, Coram explains to the consul, Dr. Lanselius, that he's trying to find his old witch friend, Serafina Pekkala. Dr. Lanselius gives him some help, explaining that Serafina Pekkala is now the queen of a witch clan near Lake Enara (*The Golden Compass*, pages 169–179).

Along the way, we learn more about the witches: that they use cloud-pine sticks for flying; that they live near the part of the world that overlaps other worlds; that they hear "immortal whispers," which we presume to be angels or the cosmic consciousness; that neither they nor their daemons feel the cold. Witches become sick with illnesses that don't affect humans, and somehow, their happiness and sadness are connected to flowers that blossom on tiny plants in the tundra (*The Golden Compass*, page 221).

While some of the witches are apparently bad, working with the people who are kidnapping children, most of the witches are on the side of good. The good witches help Farder Coram find the kidnappers.

When she meets Serafina Pekkala, Lyra marvels at the youth and beauty of the witch. Serafina has fair skin and pretty green eyes. Like all witches, she's wearing black silk and riding a cloud-pine branch. She had been Farder Coram's lover (*The Golden Compass*, pages 301–303). Serafina later explains that witches own absolutely nothing, that they don't have or need money, that they are impossible to insult, that they help each other without question. She is three hundred years old, and the oldest witch is almost a thousand years old. *Her* name is Yambe-Akka, and she is the kindhearted, smiling goddess of the dead (*The Golden Compass*, page 314).

The witches have children with human males: Their female offspring are witches, their male offspring are ordinary humans. One wonders about the offspring of the male children of these witches. Surely, the male offspring carry the genetic codes of their mothers. If the male offspring have female children, might these second-generation offspring be witches?

The witches do use herbs, potions, and spells, just as our folklore claims. Little flowers are used by humans to call for witch help. And the witches use hares, as well as herbs, to heal Will's wounded hand. Using magic, they're capable of becoming invisible. However, using the invisibility magic makes the witches tired, and the magic makes them unnoticed rather than truly invisible.

In our world, a witch is somebody who is highly skilled at sorcery and other magical arts. The term *witch* comes from the Middle English witche, which comes from the Old English terms wicca, wicce, and wiccian. The wicca terms imply that the person works sorcery. Today's witches often claim to be practicing the Wicca religion.

Witches use rituals, spells, herbs, hares, toads, and charms to manipulate nature, people, and inanimate objects. They talk to the spirits, they can be invisible, they can change shape, and they can heal simply by touching the person or animal that is injured. Although witches can be male, most of us think of witches as female.

Throughout history, people have feared and hated witches, thinking of them as old, mean-spirited hags who cast evil spells. The ancient Assyrians believed in sorcerers, witches, and wizards. The ancient Greek and Roman civilizations held that witches had special supernatural and magical powers, including great skill with herbs and potions. Witches in Rome brought the moon out of the sky, people thought; today, this is known as "drawing down the moon." As early as ancient Rome, people believed that witches worked with magic circles, made love potions (called philters), and called upon help from the spirits of the dead. Witches had the Evil Eye, which supposedly killed people by looking at them; a more rigorous definition of the Evil

Eye is that it works even if the witch just thinks about doing evil. I devote an entire chapter to the Evil Eye in my recent book, *The Truth Behind a Series of Unfortunate Events* (St. Martin's Press, 2004).

In addition to magic circles, drawing down the moon, flying brooms, invisibility, shapeshifting, rituals, spells, herbs, love potions, and calling upon the dead for help, witches use *familiars*: small animals or spirits who keep them company and help them with their magical deeds.

Between 1450 and 1800, the Europeans hunted, tortured, and killed witches. This was a period of massive hatred and debauchery. Hideous cruelty was justified by church-loving people who thought witches ate people, sucked the blood from humans, and had sex with devils. Witches included jugglers, magicians, soothsaying wizards, enchanters, and charmers.

Witch mania swept the continent and entered America, where the infamous Salem witch trials condemned many women and girls to their deaths. Their killers identified them as witches by finding signs on their bodies. Signs included: not crying, a mole anywhere on the body, ugliness, a lumpy body, physical or mental handicaps, poverty, a bad temper. If a woman or girl wasn't very well liked by her classmates or the townspeople, she might be considered a witch; as such, she was tortured to death, then hanged and burned. To elicit confessions from witches, families were tortured in front of the accused.

In other cultures, witches are also considered to be evil. The Navajo think that witches are greedy men and women who hurt other people due to jealousy. To become a witch, the Navajo believe, a person must commit murder, rob graves, eat corpses, hold midnight rituals, and make people sick. More on this later. For now, let's look at what witches are really like (if indeed they're real), compare them to the witches in *His Dark Materials*, and explore some of witch history and lore.

In *His Dark Materials*, the witches are in covens headed by queens. We've all heard about covens, and it's pretty common knowledge that witches have leaders. In 1324, Alice Kyteler of Kilkenny, Ireland, was accused of being part of a thirteen-witch coven. During the Middle Ages, witches were tortured until they admitted they were in covens. The covens were secret organizations that did horrible things. In 1662, the Scottish witch Isobel Gowdie told her inquisitors that the witches were organized in covines, which were like squads.

Today, many witches claim to belong to covens that have existed for many hundreds of years. The witches say that they are descendants of generations of unbroken lines of witches and wizards. For example, Sybil Leek's New Forest coven supposedly has existed for eight hundred years.

Usually, a coven has twelve members plus one male leader, who, according to witch hunters, is the devil or one of the devil's human representatives. During the Salem witch trials, which we'll discuss in a moment, testimony indicated that each coven had a *summoner* to tell the others about the next sabbat meeting; and a *maiden*, a young, beautiful girl who was the leader's escort at the sabbats. Needless to say, Ruta Skadi in *His Dark Materials* was not a male leader, much less a devil, and she didn't have a beautiful young girl as her consort.

Today's coven is a bit different from what I've just described. Typically, a modern coven meets at a sabbat, or circle, during the full moon. It also meets for eight seasonal festivals. The coven has a temple, where it meets, and the witches tend to convene in the middle of a circle that extends three miles in each direction. Member witches are supposed to live within the three-mile zones. It's unlikely that, in modern times, these rules are observed in a strict fashion.

And in today's coven, there is no male devil at the head with his beautiful, young lover. Instead, the modern coven tends to have a high priestess, who represents the witch Goddess. If a male priest is in the coven, the female priestess, or Goddess, still rules as the top authority. If a maiden is present, she's an administrative assistant rather than an erotic escort.

The high priestess teaches magic to the other witches, purifies the coven's magic circle, and communicates with the supreme witch Goddess. She is in command of the spirits and the elements, and she directs all of the main rituals, chants, and magic of the coven. In general, there are no witch queens.

The Goddess is also known as Mother Nature or the Great Mother. She has infinite fertility and is responsible for bringing forth all life in the world. She creates and destroys, she controls the elements, and she is the moon, which to witches is the source of magical power. The Goddess is the font of psychic ability and intuition. People have been worshipping the Goddess since Paleolithic times. The earliest religions prayed and made sacrifices to Mother Earth, calling her by thousands of different names. Creation theories claimed that the Goddess was a female who self-fertilized and gave rise to all beings. Many early societies had female leaders: they were matriarchal rather than patriarchal. If you've been to a museum, you've seen the sculptures of females with their reproductive aspects exaggerated. These sculptures were probably made by ancient cultures to represent Mother Earth, or the Goddess. The Cro-Magnons in the Upper Paleolithic Period, between 35,000 and 10,000 B.C., made these pagan Goddess sculptures, often now called "Venus figures." The Cro-Magnons drew pictures of childbirth on their cave walls. The Venus figure of Laussel, carved in approximately 19,000 B.C. in southern France, is painted red, and scholars suggest that the red connotes the blood of childbirth. From 4500 to 3500 B.C., people were still worshipping Venus figures, and in Africa from 7000 to 6000 B.C., the Horned Goddess, a self-fertilizing bisexual spiritual creature, was carved into cave walls. Ancient Egypt had its Goddess, as well, in the form of Ta-Urt, the Great One, who was a pregnant hippopotamus. In 4000 B.C., Sumeria's queen and princesses were associated with the Goddess, while its king and princes were associated with a god.

Between 1800 and 1500 B.C., when Abraham lived in Canaan, the worship of the Goddess began to decline. Later the Church denounced pagan cults and religions that were based on the Goddess, as well. During the Middle Ages, the pagan Goddess called Diana was flourishing, and the Church repressed worship of Diana as worship of a pagan deity.

Diana was a goddess of the moon and remains one of the most significant figures in modern witchcraft. She's a feminist Goddess, emphasizing independence, self-esteem, aggressive behavior, and positive attributes associated with worship of the moon. She is the modern patron Goddess of all witches.

Today's Goddess is closely associated with Gaia, the living consciousness of Earth, named after the Greek Goddess of Earth. Of course, *His Dark Materials* emphasizes the consciousness of not only Earth but of all planets, stars, and everything else in the universe. It is a key concept in the trilogy.

Clearly, life on Earth influences the planet in many ways. Each life-form affects the others; animals impact plants and vice versa; the environment supports directly affected by what creatures do here on Earth. The planet supports a complex web of life and inanimate objects: rocks, clouds, the air: all are intertwined with humans, animals, and plants in a complex feedback system. If Earth is alive, as espoused by the concept of Gaia, and we move a bush from this planet to another, that bush probably would die. The bush must be on the living planet, or Gaia, of Earth to live; and possibly, this is why Will can't survive in the long run on Lyra's world, and Lyra can't survive for long in his world.

In *His Dark Materials*, the Dust is cosmic consciousness and forms everything throughout the universe. The Dust parallels the modern idea of Gaia, or consciousness of planet Earth. If the Earth is conscious and alive, it follows that the other planets, the stars, the moons, and so forth, might be alive as well. The Dust links all living and nonliving things together in a complex web. The *mulefa's* relationships with seed pods and giant trees are based on Dust, which the *mulefa* call sraf.

So the Goddess of the witches, in reality, fits into the concepts of Dust, *mulefa*, Gaia, and witches in *His Dark Materials*.

We've already mentioned how beautiful and young the witches are in *His Dark Materials*. But in reality, at least until the modern day, witches have been known for their ugliness and old age. In fact, the word *hag* originated with the Goddess myths of pagan Europeans and ancient Greeks, Egyptians, and Celts. In ancient Egypt, for example, a *heq* was a matriarchal ruler with magical powers. In ancient Greece, Hecate was the Goddess of witchcraft. In Norse mythology, Hel was the death-Goddess of sorcery.

However, good hags abound in some Irish and Scottish myths. These good hags are beautiful and young, as in *His Dark Materials*. And in the sixteenth century, hags and fairies often referred to the same beings. In late-night fairy rings, the fairies and witches would party and trade secrets about magic.

But for the most part, hags remain ugly, old witches. In Great Britain, hags worked with dead spirits and bogeymen to hurt people and animals. The Celtic hag Black Annis was a cannibal derived from the Goddess, and she ate people and animals whenever she sneaked out of her cave in the Dane Hills.

I'm not sure why anyone would want to be known as a hag. Yet in modern times, many young women want to be known as witches. I suspect it makes them feel cool to think that they have supernatural powers, and maybe some of them really do. Who am I to say?

Those who want to be witches today must be initiated into a

coven. In *His Dark Materials*, it sufficed to be born into a witch family. As long as you were female and your mother was a witch, then you were destined to be a witch.

From a classical perspective, the initiation into a coven involves suffering, symbolic death, and symbolic rebirth as a witch. Initiation means that a person is allowed to participate in a secret society; in this case, a witch coven.

Of course, during the witch-hunt madness of the Middle Ages, people figured that witch initiations involved murder, eating other people, and various other obscenities. The Devil presided over the initiation ceremony, which, of course, took place deep in the night in mysterious, remote locations. The new witches renounced the Christian faith, gave their Bibles to the Devil, and recited blasphemous oaths that denounced God, Christ, Mary, the saints, heaven, earth, and all other traditional aspects of Christianity. They swore their lives to the Devil, and then he baptized them with evil, new names and scratched or bit them. At the end of the vile ceremonies, the Devil made the people take off their clothes, and then he gave familiars (small animals and spirits) to them as helpmates and recorded their witch names in his black book. Sacrifices of animals were made, and then all the witches went wild with obscene dancing and the eating of roasted humans.

Clearly, modern witchcraft doesn't require initiations that involve the Devil, cannibalism, or orgies. People engaging in these types of activities would probably end up in jail—maybe for life. Today, witchcraft is a pseudo-religion that does *not* require denouncing Christianity, worshipping the Devil, or killing anyone. After a year and one day, a woman is initiated into a coven by a high priest. The ceremony occurs in a magic circle. And then, it's almost like moving up the ranks of scouting: The new witch advances by learning rituals, spells, and the history of the occult.

Except that it's not that simple, and it's definitely not that "clean." The new witch is blindfolded. She's also tied by ropes, then whipped with cords. The coven gives her a set of magical tools and a new witch name.

After proving herself a loyal member of the coven, the new witch must undergo a second initiation act. This one is very similar to the first, except that she's now "given" the magical powers of the person who is initiating her.

The third initiation ceremony is worse. Magical tools are used on the witch in some sort of sexual ritual. And then, the witches dance and eat for hours: though orgies and cannibalism are not common.

We've mentioned the word *elements* several times. These elements—earth, air, water, and fire—are central to witchcraft and are aligned with the four points of the magical circle. They are also closely aligned with spirits known as elementals: earth elementals are called gnomes; air elementals are called sylphs; water elementals are undines; and fire elementals are salamanders.

The gnomes may be dryads, hamadryads (or tree spirits), brownies, elves, satyrs, pans, or goblins. They're concerned mainly with rocks, stones, plants, minerals, and gems. When working with animals or humans, they handle the bones. If betrayed, earth elementals, or gnomes, are vengeful and cause a lot of trouble. Lore has it that gnomes guard treasures, such as pots of gold.

The water elementals are made up of the undines, water sprites, mermaids, sea nymphs, and such strange-sounding creatures as limoniades, nereides, potamides, oreades, and naiads. As you may have guessed, they create ocean waves and guard other bodies of water such as lakes and rivers. Witches believe that a water elemental guards each fountain, each creek, each spurt of water. They're physically beautiful beings, most often considered female, and they often take on human form to communicate and interact with people.

The air elementals, or sylphs and fairies, cast the winds and make the snow and clouds. Sometimes they cause dreams, and within humans and animals, they work within the realms of the nervous system. Generally, the sylphs and fairies are happy spirits, dancing in the grass and on the flowers, and they tend to be generous and kind.

The fire elementals, or salamanders, are directly responsible for fire: Without the elementals, fire cannot be created. Within humans and animals, they work within the realms of the bloodstream and the liver, and they affect human emotions. Salamanders either look like lizards or tiny balls of light in the middle of a flame.

Some elementals are created by witches simply by thinking; these elementals perform deeds and then disappear. It's as if "real" witches are collecting and condensing Dust to do their will. Other elementals are found in nature in the form of spirits bound to animals, rocks, insects, plants, and so forth. This type of elemental is ruled by the Archangels, described in Chapter 3.

The elements themselves are derived from ancient beliefs, such as the categories of all beings devised by Plato: earth and pedestrians; air and birds; water and fish; and fire and stars. Occultists believe they must rule all the elements before mastering the spiritual realm.

The witches' familiars are sources of elemental energy, and the witches bless their ritual tools with the four elements. Even the magic circle is consecrated using the four elements. The center binding all elements is the connection between the witches and the cosmic consciousness.

Once again, it's striking to note the similarity of ideas in *His Dark Materials* to ideas that have been in the minds of men for thousands of years. As with Gaia, the witch circles, and the beliefs about the elements—everything is alive in nature and rooted by a cosmic consciousness—pervades human mythology and folklore, as well as *His Dark Materials*.

However, the witches in *His Dark Materials* aren't seen within their circles. We can only assume that they meet in circles, given that so much else about them is the same as what we believe about witches here on Earth. Sure, there are differences—the witches in *His Dark Materials* are young and beautiful, they're kind and generous; but for the most part, the similarities prevail: They fly on sticks, they cast spells, they use magic herbs, and so forth.

A witch circle represents a boundary in which concentrated magical power presides. The circle is a gateway to the gods, or to cosmic consciousness, and symbolizes the wholeness of the universe.

In ancient times, witches drew circles around sick people and newborn babies to protect them from the devil. Pagan stone circles are still found throughout England.

Witches must follow specific instructions when creating their circles. The circle must be drawn only during a particular time of day, and only if astrological conditions permit. A consecrated tool must be used. Before drawing a circle on it, a floor must be thoroughly scrubbed, and sometimes the witches sprinkle salt to define where the perimeter will be located. Most circles are nine feet in diameter. When drawing the circle, the head witch moves clockwise, to represent the movement of the moon and other cosmic entities in the sky; to create a circle for negative magic, the witch moves counterclockwise. At this point, the witch consecrates the circle using the four elements, and she asks the spirits to protect the circle from demons.

The north quarter of the circle is associated with great power, darkness, and mystery. Because pagans often built their temples facing the North Star, the north became associated with the Christian Devil. Northern doors in ancient European churches are often called "the Devil's door." Christian ceremonies are rarely held on the northern sides of churches.

The south quarter of the circle is associated with the channeling of energy created by nature and psychic will. This area of the circle represents the sun, the element of fire, and the magic wand.

The east quarter represents illumination and enlightenment, and is associated with the sword and the element of air. The altar usually faces east, and quite often, witches think that spiritual consciousness resides mainly in this quarter.

The final quarter, the west, represents fertility and emotions. It's associated with the chalice.

The altar, often placed inside the circle, is where the witches make offerings and hold ceremonies. It is associated with the Goddess, Gaia, or Mother Earth. Few requirements, oddly enough, are mandated when constructing the altar. One rule is that iron and steel should not be used, as these metals interfere with the magic energies created by ritual tools made from metal.

On the altar, the witches place various objects of worship. The black-handled, double-edged, six-inch athame knife directs energy and represents the element of fire. As a main ritual tool, it is used to carve or draw the magic circle, and invoke and release the powers within the quarters. It is rarely used to cut anything other than a tiny doorway in the circle so people can pass into the circle; or a ritual cake, bread, or cord. The white-handled, double-edged, six-inch bolline (or boleen) knife is used to cut magical items such as herbs and to carve runes. The sword, like the athame, represents the element of air. The peyton is a disk with a pentacle on its face. Its place is at the center of the altar, where it represents the female aspect of life. The wand represents the element of fire, and may be used in place of the athame to draw the circle and invoke the quarters. Of course, the magic wand is used when casting spells. The staff, a long version of the wand, is used to direct energy. The labrys, or double-headed axe, is also used to direct energy. Also on the altar are various crystals, oils, salt, water, wine, and bells; as well as statues and images of the gods. A thurible, or incense burner, is also located on the altar, and the incense purifies the air within the sacred space. Cauldrons and brooms are placed next to the altar in convenient locations should they be needed during the magical ceremonies.

The book of shadows is a modern tome that ancient witches didn't use. In the book are all the herbal remedies, spells, chants, dances, rules, rituals, and other material related to witchcraft. There is no one book of shadows corresponding to a witches' bible. Indeed, each coven may have its own book of shadows. The witches in *His Dark Materials* do not refer to these sorts of books before casting spells and creating herbal remedies.

We'll touch on a few more items related to witches in general, and then turn to a little witch lore. First, let's ponder whether witches can fly. As noted, the witches in *His Dark Materials* ride cloud-pine branches.

When on trial, many witches claimed that they were able to fly because they rubbed magical ointments on their bodies and brooms. Deadly nightshade is often considered one of the main ingredients in these ointments. The nightshade contains tropane alkaloids that are absorbed quickly through the skin. Two of the alkaloids, scopolamine and hyoscyamine, produce intense hallucinations.

In Mexico, people who ingest nightshade report vivid sensations of flying. They actually believe that they soar to distant lands through the skies.

So it's quite conceivable that witches who rub their bodies with nightshade ointments do indeed think that they're flying. (Centuries ago, this type of behavior wasn't all that strange. Especially when you consider that Italian women once daubed their eyes with rinses made of atropine, an alkaloid containing deadly nightshade. The atropine made their eyes look dreamy and beautiful.[69]

Ancient European folk legends tell of the goddess who travels through the night sky, often accompanied by spirits of the dead. The German goddess was known as Holda, and she was kind, even responsible for the birth of children. Father Christmas, or Santa Claus, rides the skies to this day, giving goodies and toys to children.

But for the most part, as time marched forward, the women who flew with the goddesses no longer were considered kind. The ancient legend of the flying, hideous, bird-woman, somewhat like a harpy (whom we discuss in Chapter 7), became more rooted in human lore. This bird-woman, called the Strix, flew at night and ate human flesh. Possibly, she originated from the Dark Goddess.

In addition, other stories about flying women grew. These flying witches knew herbal magic and could cast evil spells that destroyed the chastity of the very young and brought the dead back to life.

In the 1500s, witches were drawn and painted riding shovels, sticks, and even demons. In the 1600s, they were shown riding brooms and demons. The broom supposedly swept the tracks of the witch from the sky as she rode. Isobel Gowdie, "a famous Scottish witch of the 17th century, claimed to use her broom not for travel but to deceive her husband. Prior to going to a sabbat, she substituted her broom for herself in bed. He never knew the difference, she said, which might have been more of a comment on their marriage than a confession of witchcraft."[70]

69. Kevin Short, "How Witches Fly High," http://www.unsolvedmysteries.com/usm 169177.html. Also see Jani Farrell Roberts, "Did Witches Really Fly?" at http://www .witch.plus.com/7day-extracts/witches-flying.html.
70. Rosemary Ellen Guiley, *The Encyclopedia of Witches & Witchcraft*. New York: Checkmark Books, 1999, p. 35. If you're interested in details about all aspects of witchcraft, this is a great book to explore. Highly recommended!

Another aspect of "real" witchcraft that the witches in *His Dark Materials* use is shapeshifting. They can turn into other people, animals, birds, and other forms of life. When flying up chimneys, witches supposedly can change themselves into smaller creatures such as wolves, cats, hares, and bats.

In *His Dark Materials*, the witches wear black silk: how chic! Long, ugly black robes are generally associated with witches in the real world. Black supposedly conducts energy well, and some witches give this reason as an "excuse" for wearing black. Personally, I think that black simply is associated with matters of the occult: black cats, black-robed witches, black moods, black (evil) witches versus white (kind) witches. But more important, when meeting at night sabbats, back when witches were considered evil enough to torture and kill, a black robe helped the witch fade into the night.

As for spells, drawing down the moon is one of the most important modern rituals. In this ritual, a coven's high priestess becomes the Goddess and then utters spiritual poetry and other beautiful chants. The spells themselves are the words required to make something happen. They are also known as incantations, chants, charms, and runes. The rituals are actions that must be performed in specific order while the witch utters the spells.

It's interesting to note that cultures all over the world have witch mythologies dating back to ancient times. As with most subjects, such as angels and God, which we discussed already, the witches in *His Dark Materials* tend to possess attributes normally associated with witches in Christianity.

But where do all the other witches fit into *His Dark Materials*? Surely there are other cultures on the billions of worlds, just as we share different cultures on our world.

In Africa, witch doctors have long been a part of the landscape. Witchcraft is known by the Nyakyusa as "python in the belly," by the Pondo as "snake of the women," and by the Xhosa as "great hairy beast." The Tswana believe in night witches as well as day sorcerers. The night witches are elderly women who cast evil spells on people. The day sorcerers use herbs and potions to inflict harm.

In China, witchcraft is favored by a culture steeped in mysticism and magic. Herbs, the staff, potions, and hares are all used in rituals that are associated with the moon.

Indian witchcraft has existed for centuries and includes amulets, charms, and potions. On the South Pacific islands, magic predominates, with many different gods, spirits, and supernatural beliefs. The sea plays a central role in magic, and the people routinely cast spells.

In Norway, witches were found guilty of causing shipwrecks and murder. In the Basque region of the Pyrenees, six hundred witches were tortured and killed in four months.

Between 1576 and 1612 in Austria, witchcraft flourished under Emperor Rudolf II. He decided that all insane people were really witches. If a little kid said you were a witch, it sufficed for crazy Emperor Rudolf II to have you killed as a witch. In Salzburg, a witchcraft scare cost a hundred people their lives after brutal torture. In Tyrol, only children under the age of seven were safe from accusations of witchcraft. Those accused were tortured mercilessly.

Witches didn't fare much better in Bavaria, England, France, Germany, Italy, Spain, Sweden, Scotland, or America. In fact, torture and death became commonplace around the world for witches. In 1641, England made witchcraft a capital crime. In 1688, the Salem witch trials began with the hanging of laundress Goody Glover, who was accused of turning Martha Goodwin and her younger brother and two sisters into witches. In 1692, nineteen witches were tortured and hanged, one wizard (a male witch) was pressed to death, and four accused witches died in prison.

Luckily for the witches in *His Dark Materials*, they're considered kind, benevolent, helpful creatures. Rather than wear coarse, shapeless black robes, they wear fragments of black silk. Rather than have giant noses with warts, they have beautiful features and hair, with youthful bodies and grace. These are sweet creatures, who have children with men rather than demons. There's not going to be a Lapland Witch Trial anytime soon.

DAEMONS

Daemons are a key component of *His Dark Materials*. Directly linked to the cosmic consciousness made up of dark matter aka Dust, the daemons are physical beings who happen to be souls. Each person has a daemon. In Lyra's world, the daemons are separate beings, physically apart from their humans; but in Will's world, the daemons are "silent voices in the mind and no more" (*The Subtle Knife*, page 214).

Operating as a soul that provides advice, the daemon talks to its human, is a lifetime companion and best friend. For example, in the beginning of *The Golden Compass* (page 9), "Lyra felt a mixture of thoughts contending in her head, and she would have liked nothing better than to share them with her daemon, but she was proud too. Perhaps she should try to clear them up without out his help." Not only does the daemon talk aloud in the human's native tongue—which is a universal language throughout the billions of parallel worlds—but the daemon can also use mental telepathy to communicate with its human. For example, during a kidnapping scene, Pantalaimon "thinks" to Lyra that she shouldn't worry, which instantly relaxes her (*The Golden Compass*, page 281).

The daemon can change shape constantly, as long as the person remains a child. As soon as a human enters puberty, the daemon starts to solidify into one static form that represents the personality and character of its human. For example, if a human is peaceful, her daemon may be a dove; if the adult human is playful, the daemon may be a kitten forever. When Lyra and Roger go into the crypt beneath the oratory, they find generations of masters, each in a coffin with a brass plaque bearing an image: ". . . this one a basilisk, this a serpent, this a monkey. She realized they were images of the dead men's daemons. As people became adult, their daemons lost the power to change and assumed one shape, keeping it permanently" (*The Golden Compass*, pages 48–49).

Lyra's daemon, Pantalaimon, appears as a moth, ermine, lion, wildcat, sparrow, and canary, to name only a few shapes. Pantalaimon prefers to sleep as an ermine around Lyra's neck; he's a lion when trying to frighten a night-ghast; a wildcat when he and Lyra are escaping from Mrs. Coulter in London; and a sparrow as he wanders alone.

Lord Asriel's daemon is the snow leopard, Stelmaria, and Mrs. Coulter's daemon is a golden monkey. All servants have daemons who are in the shapes of dogs.

Pantalaimon, like most other daemons, is the opposite gender of his human. Males have female daemons, and vice versa.

When the gyptian children are fighting, their daemons join in—with claws, paws, teeth, and snarls—and battle each other. Later, Pantalaimon fights Mrs. Coulter's golden monkey daemon, and Pantalaimon professes to hate the monkey (*The Golden Compass*, page 86). Not only do the daemons fight each other to protect their humans, they also operate as scouts, skulking ahead, lurking around corners, making sure everything's safe before their humans proceed. For example, Tillerman's, Farder Coram's, and Lyra's daemons "[scout] the corners ahead, watching behind, listening for the slightest footfall" (*The Golden Compass*, page 157).

But if a human tries to touch somebody else's daemon, society considers this to be a gross breach of etiquette. "Daemons might touch each other, of course, or fight; but the prohibition against human-daemon contact went so deep that even in battle no warrior would touch an enemy's daemon. It was utterly forbidden" (*The Golden Compass*, page 142). And later, when a kidnapper (Lyra is kidnapped often!) picks up Pantalaimon, the daemon is "shaking, nearly out of his mind with horror and disgust" (*The Golden Compass*, page 275).

Daemons have other, very physical, creature habits. For example, the smell of cedarwood puts them to sleep.

When a human dies, so does his daemon, or soul. This is unlike what many people believe in our world, whereby when we die, our souls go to heaven (or elsewhere, say, to hell). And in *His Dark Materials*, when a daemon dies, so does its human. Some of the humans then wander like zombies, others simply die on the spot. We'll discuss this topic in more detail later.

Given that the daemon is a soul, it would be horrific to have it removed from the human. But that's exactly what *His Dark Materials* is about: Mrs. Coulter and the Church want to cut the daemons from the children *before* they reach puberty. They think that it is the soul that makes a person commit the sin of physical love, the original sin that caused the fall of Adam and Eve, hence bringing about the desperation, greed, and evil nature of man ever since.

As early as *The Golden Compass*, Lord Asriel shows a lantern slide of a man with light streaming all around him. Next to the man is a severed child: only part of him showing in the light. We learn quickly that the light is coming from another world, a city viewed within the Northern Lights, or Aurora Borealis. Lord Asriel says that the child is severed, and Lyra realizes that he means that the child has been "cut" (*The Golden Compass*, page 60).

Later, Lyra and a witch's goose daemon enter a building and find the daemons of the "cut" children. The daemons are in glass cases on shelves, and they look like ghosts of their former selves. Being souls cut from their humans, all of them are terrified and many are weeping. Some are already dead: simply gone from their cases. Sadly, although Lyra and the goose daemon are able to free the remaining ghostlike daemons, as the goose comments, once a daemon is cut from its human, it can never be part of the human again (*The Golden Compass*, page 259–261). The humans wander like zombies, or simply die. The zombie looks and behaves like a dead person. As Lyra comments, a zombie is "a person without their daemon!" (*The Golden Compass*, page 375).

Further, if a human enters another world, its daemon cannot live its full life. The daemon will die unless it's in the world where it was born. Of course, the daemon can last for a short number of years in other worlds, but in time, not only will the daemon die, but so will its human (*The Amber Spyglass*, page 363). This fact is a key to the end of the series, where Lyra and Will must split up and live in their own respective worlds.

Witches have daemons too, but in their case, the daemons can be far apart from them. In the case of humans, the daemon must remain very close, or else both human and daemon suffer great despair and physical longing. "Everyone tested it when they were growing up: seeing how far they could pull apart [from their daemon], coming back with intense relief" (*The Golden Compass*, page 195). Witches send their daemons long distances to operate as scouts, convey information, and basically, to be spies (*The Golden Compass*, page 164).

Because they aren't humanoid, the armored talking bears

don't have daemons. In fact, King Iofur of the bears desperately wants a daemon and keeps a daemon-doll on his lap at all times.

It was René Descartes who first wrote the famous line, "I think, therefore I am." Descartes was referring to the human ability to consider itself as a distinct individual, a self with a soul. But what is the soul, the self, the mind?

According to Plato, the gods inserted souls into our bodies. These souls were "of another nature,"[71] and inside digestive systems were "the part of the soul which desires meats and drinks and the other things of which it has need by reason of the bodily nature."[72]

Aristotle assumed that all objects consist of matter, and that the forms of objects change as this matter changes. For example, a house consists of stones, and when someone takes the stones apart, the house changes form. So to Aristotle, the soul is the "form" that a creature takes, and it takes care of and consists of everything that the creature does to stay alive. Aristotle thought that creatures other than humans also have souls; that each type of creature has a different type of soul. A different set of conditions is required to keep a tiger alive than a human, for example. However, he did think that the human soul differed from the animal soul in that the human soul was *rational* and included reason and will: the mind, the self, the consciousness.

Aristotle attempted to classify all these souls by dissecting animals, though he didn't (as far as we know) dissect humans. He was looking for the place where souls reside. He postulated that the soul lived inside the heart yet affected the entire body. The nervous system was largely unknown in Aristotle's time, and

71. James Longrigg, *Greek Rational Medicine: Philosophy and Medicine from Alchaeon to the Alexandrians*. New York: Routledge Press, 1993, p. 58.
72. Andrew Cunningham, *The Anatomical Renaissance: The Resurrection of the Anatomical Projects of the Ancients*. Aldershot, United Kingdom: Ashgate, 1997, p. 12.

so he believed that the eyes and ears were connected to blood vessels rather than to the brain. Because the blood vessels were, of course, connected to the heart, he figured that the heart controlled our senses as well as all movement.

In 322 B.C., Greek anatomists Herophilus and Erasistratus dissected human corpses and discovered the nervous system. They realized that a system existed inside the body beyond the one controlled by the heart. Rather, the nervous system had to do with the spine and skull. And of course Herophilus and Erasistratus formed their own hypotheses about the soul. They believed that the soul came into the body with each breath. Once inside the body, the soul flowed into the heart and coursed through the arteries. Some of this life force traveled into the brain. Further, they believed that the mind was housed in chambers of the heart. From the heart, the mind flowed to the muscles and brain, and the brain itself had no control over the body.

Four hundred years later, in A.D. 150, the doctor Galen arrived in Alexandria to study the research of Herophilus and Erasistratus. Galen had access to remarkable specimens: He served as a doctor to gladiators. In addition, he dissected animals every day. He eventually combined the teachings of Aristotle, Plato, Herophilus, Erasistratus, and Hippocrates into new theories, and he actually wound up serving as the doctor to emperors.

Galen suggested that each organ had a special purification role in the body. The stomach attracted food and turned it into chyle, which moved to the intestines and liver. Then the liver transformed chyle into blood, which flowed to the heart. The lungs attracted all the impurities from the blood, and from the liver, the purified blood went into the veins. Meanwhile, inside the heart, some of the blood mixed with air from the lungs. This blood contained "vital spirits" and flowed throughout the body, including the brain. At the base of the skull, the blood was further purified and turned into "animal spirits" that created thoughts and sensory experiences. The "animal spirits" also enabled the body to move. Basically, Galen thought of the brain as a pump at the top of the body, while the mind was stuffed into all the empty space inside the skull. He also suggested that the human mind existed in the stars, the moon, and the sun, which all had intelligence far beyond our own. You might say that Galen believed in a cosmic consciousness.

After Galen died, Christianity absorbed a lot of his medical theories, particularly those about the soul and the mind. In the Old Testament, the soul lives in the blood and is life. It dies when the human dies. In the New Testament, the soul is immortal and will face either eternal bliss or eternal hell. In the early church, the Old Testament soul lived in the heart and liver, while the New Testament soul was invisible and lived nowhere and everywhere all at once, while somehow having special facilities inside the skull.

But the church derived views about the soul from sources other than Galen. In particular, the church still believed some of what Aristotle taught, that the soul lives inside the heart.

Much later, as scientists discovered atoms, the Greek philosopher Epicurus suggested that the world consisted of invisible particles that controlled almost everything. Perhaps the gods didn't care about humans at all; only the particles mattered. In addition, Epicurus postulated that the soul was made of atoms inside the chest, and these soul atoms seeped from our bodies, only to be restored as we breathed. The soul was, in essence, a cosmic property. When the soul seeped from the body but breath no longer replenished the soul atoms, that was the point wherein the human body died.

Of course, religious people were quite upset by the idea of a soul that doesn't survive human death. In fact, Dante went so far as to put Epicurus into hell.

Along came Thomas Aquinas in the thirteenth century.

Aquinas ignored Epicurus's claim that atoms and cosmic souls existed. Instead, the theologian suggested that the stars were a twinkling of heaven, where all good souls lived forever after the body died. Aquinas supported Aristotle's idea that the soul resides in the heart and is the "form" of all life. Aquinas also taught that the soul's facilities were in the skull. Further, of all the animal souls, only the human soul survived death.

While Aquinas set the stage for natural philosophy in universities, medical doctors continued to teach Galen's anatomy, stripping off skin and skull to study the human body. Medical students learned that the soul resided in the heart, the liver, and the skull. Invisible spirits aka the immortal soul coursed throughout the body along visible pathways—arteries, nervous system, digestive system.

In 1537, Andreas Vesalius, in charge of surgery and anatomy lectures at the University of Padua, used cadavers in the lab to teach students about the human body. Vesalius made huge, detailed charts of the human body. He realized that Galen's ideas about human anatomy weren't based on dissections of human cadavers. Instead, Galen's human anatomy had been based on dissections of other animals. Vesalius ended up compiling the first detailed atlas of human anatomy; it was called *De humani corporis fabrica libri septem*, or *Seven Books on the Structure of the Human Body*. It included pictures of the dissected brain. He concluded that perhaps animal spirits didn't flow through the brain, after all; perhaps the soul didn't trickle up from the heart, course through the skull, and derive its facilities from the brain. Afraid of causing an uproar, he suggested but didn't push the idea that the brain itself was the seat of the soul or mind.

As late as 1600, people still believed that the soul was in the heart, liver, and skull, and that it somehow was everywhere and nowhere. The chambers of the heart controlled the body and mind. In addition, each person was linked to the four elements of earth, water, fire, and air, which also made up the stars, the moon, the sun, and even the demons that could cause a man to go mad.

These ideas were more widespread than you might imagine. Doctors healed patients by flushing bad spirits from their bodies. Laxatives, vomiting, and bleeding were all used, as well as astrology to determine when the doctor should flush bad spirits from the patient's body. Horoscopes, charms and amulets, religious sermons, and prayers were all used by doctors attempting to restore a natural balance of the four elements to the body.

But as this strange form of medicine boomed, so did new ideas about religion, philosophy, and the soul. People began thinking that the entire world was a living thing (this philosophy is called Gaia) and that the human soul was part of a cosmic soul. This cosmic soul could influence events, give people ideas, help make people happy, ruin someone's life. Again, we're struck by the similarity between this view of a cosmic consciousness and the view that Philip Pullman gives us in *His Dark Materials*. This new philosophy was called natural magic.

Of course, the official church disapproved of natural magic. It smacked of witches and pagan religions. The church insisted that the soul is immortal and special in each person.

The battle raged on: religious soul versus scientific mind.

In most religions, God is an omniscient presence, a mind, if you will, with infinite knowledge. Yet, is God's mind a disembodied brain? Nobody believes that, anymore than they believe that souls are minds that are floating through outer space.

Our physical brains may very well be the same thing as our minds: our thoughts. In other words, the neurocircuitry in the physical flesh may combine in highly intricate ways to form our thoughts; another entity, a spiritual mind, may not enter into the picture. While some scientists believe this to be the case, that brain and mind are one, others believe the opposite.

Regardless, our thoughts are clearly coupled tightly to our

brains and bodies. When our senses detect pain or heat, our minds know what we're feeling. In fact, our minds—our thoughts—receive a steady stream of information from our senses. We then develop new thoughts or reshape existing ones. For example, say you're reading this book (not too hard to imagine, I suppose), and suddenly you hear a loud crash. You think that perhaps a tree branch has fallen on the roof. But the noise wasn't that close, you think, so perhaps it was a car or truck backfiring on the road. The physical world outside your body has affected your senses (hearing, in this case), thus causing your mind to consider new thoughts.

Conversely, your mind can affect the physical environment. Continuing our example, you get up from the easy chair (bed or sofa, wherever you're reading this book) to determine the source of the loud crash. Your arms move, you mark your place in the book, you put the book down, you leave the house or apartment, you look at the roof, you look up and down the street. Your thoughts have affected your physical environment: They've made you move, put down a book, go outside, investigate the area. Indeed, human thoughts are responsible for shaping the physical world: the buildings, chairs, beds, sofas, books, etc.

The interesting aspect of this consideration is when we start to ponder where matter acts upon the mind, and where the mind acts upon matter. How are the two correlated?

When the loud crash occurs, it sends sound waves to your ear drum, which vibrates and sends information to the cochlea, where a membrane sends the vibration information to a fluid in your inner ear. The fluid causes some electric impulses to go flying down your auditory nerves into your brain. At this point, your brain registers that you have heard a sound. You *think*, I have a heard a sound, and it's loud. You even draw conclusions about what might have caused the sound. Your mind is working. Then, involving even more complex neurochemical transmissions, your mind makes a decision: You will put down the book, go outside, and search for the source of the sound. You may be worried. Was the noise an accident? Has someone been hurt? Could it be your friend next door? Why, you just saw him yesterday, and the two of you have been friends since you were two years old. Worry and fear intermingle with potential sorrow about losing your friend.

Note that another person may react in an entirely different way. A lazy sloth won't care if his friend's been crushed by a fallen helicopter next door. A maniac will be happy to think that some horrible calamity has befallen the little old lady across the street.

The material scientist might tell himself that, should we ever know exactly how the brain is wired, we'll be able to figure out why you react as you do, why the sloth doesn't care, why the maniac is filled with joy—all by the same event. It all boils down to neurotransmissions. There is no mind, no self, no thought process that can't be explained by physics.

However, let's consider further that each person may respond in an entirely different way to the same set of events. Each person uses *free will* to determine whether and how he will respond to the loud crash. Our souls, our minds, require free will to operate. How does free will function within the laws of physics, which are rigid deterministic laws? Circuits supposedly operate in fixed ways: if A happens, do B; if B happens, trigger C and D. Is it possible that the mind plumbs the depths of brain cells and nerves to create the neurotransmissions that enable us to create new ideas, make decisions based on personal morals and private memories? Is the mental truly part of the physical brain, or does the mental operate in conjunction with—but separate from—the physical brain?

In *His Dark Materials*, we're told that consciousness arose at some point, long ago, in human history. And it was at that moment that Dust aka dark matter took over. We could assume that free will, the ability to be an individual self with an individual soul, is the force of consciousness. We don't know if monkeys are conscious (I believe they are), if worms, computers, and dogs are conscious. We don't know if a human baby is conscious an hour before birth, or three months before birth. Just when does a human become conscious? And who's to say that our dogs and cats aren't conscious and operating with free will? It's possible that consciousness formed a long time ago in the evolving brain, just as Philip Pullman suggests in *His Dark Materials*.

We can't actually *touch* someone else's consciousness. We can interact with our own consciousness, just as Lyra interacts with her daemon. But nobody else is allowed to touch Pantalaimon.

As noted earlier, in ancient times the soul was a life force of some kind, possibly rooted in the pits of our stomachs, in our hearts, in our brains. This life animated us, put the breath into our bodies. In the New Testament, the soul is somewhat analogous to the idea of self or mind. According to the *New Catholic Encyclopedia*, the soul is "the source of thought activity."[73] It is an entity, much as Lyra's daemon is an entity separate from her body. This is the dualist theory of the body and mind (soul), developed by Descartes and introduced in Chapter 2 of this book.

According to the dualist theory, we consist of a physical body and a soul or mind. The body is the host receptacle for the soul/mind. Descartes believed that the soul is based in the brain's pineal gland. It is through the pineal gland that the ephemeral mind interacts with the physical body.

As shamans and other spiritual seekers study, starve, and pray, it's possible for their souls to be released from the prisons of their bodies. In death, the soul is released to ultimate freedom. This is similar to the concept of ghosts in *His Dark Materials*. In the trilogy, the ghosts survive the death of both body and dae-

73. *New Catholic Encyclopedia*. New York: McGraw-Hill, 1967, p. 460.

mon/soul; and at the end of *The Amber Spyglass*, Lyra and Will are able to free the poor ghosts from endless purgatory, so the ghosts can dissipate with glee into the sky and melt back into the universal cosmic consciousness.

While the soul can reside outside the brain (or outside the body, in the case of daemons), it is connected to the body *through* the brain. The daemons communicate with humans constantly, and often use mental telepathy. Some philosophers have pegged the human body as a machine, with the soul guiding it. The soul is invisible and has no size or weight. If the human body is an engine, the soul has often been called "the ghost in the machine."[74]

If the soul is an invisible ghost, we're left to wonder *where it is*. Does it just float through the air surrounding our bodies? Does it cruise inside our bodies? Is it far away in outer space? Is it in some fold of spacetime, yet locked into the grids of our bodies? And if the soul has substance, then we are left with similar questions: *Where and what is it*?

If the soul is the essence of who we are, does it exist after our bodies die? Why would it? And how does the air around us contain the billions and billions of souls that were once attached to live humans? And where is the soul before we're born? Does it exist, or does it come into being the moment a human is born?

Now you're probably thinking that I'm suggesting that souls don't exist, but I'm not taking sides or expressing a personal opinion. If the soul is an abstract concept that can't be proven, this doesn't imply that the soul is not real. It only implies that we don't know enough about the human brain and mind to know if the soul exists.

74. Originally by G. Ryle in *The Concept of Mind*, New York: Hutchinson, 1949, though the phrase "ghost in the machine" has become a common term in many texts and articles.

Okay, you've caught me: I'm avoiding expressing personal opinions about God, angels, daemons and souls, heaven, and hell in this book. As stated earlier, I'm not a religious expert; I'm only a science and science fiction writer. I do believe that the soul is another word for the mind or consciousness; that the soul is an integral part of our physical brains; that what constitutes "self" is a complex mix of neural biology and neurotransmissions. It's interesting to wonder how the soul can be physically distinct from us, why it must remain near (except for witches), and why its death means our death, and vice versa. A "life force" is unnecessary for matter to become animate. A soul is unnecessary for matter to become conscious. I have a hard time trying to determine exactly how physically separate daemons might affect brain chemistry to such a large extent. Again, the caveat: These are personal opinions.

Still, I also note that, until proven otherwise, I can't discount the possibility that the soul exists as a separate entity.

After Descartes, a doctor named Thomas Willis started working on theories about the brain, the nerves, and the soul, among other things. Willis had some strange theories about the brain, but he pushed neuroscience strongly in the right direction. He suggested that blood entered the brain, where the natural spirits were distilled from it. Once inside the brain, the spirits traveled through the nerves and escaped from the body in the form of vapor. Willis eventually led a project to unlock the secret places of man's mind. How was he going to do it? By surgically exploring the brain.

Rather than slicing off pieces of the brain, Willis removed whole brains from the skull, and he realized that the brain had several distinct parts. He saw the marrow at the base of the brain, where the spinal cord connected to the brain; this area is now called the medulla oblongata. Above the medulla oblongata is the cerebellum, which looks like a ball, and then above both the medulla oblongata and the cerebellum is the cerebrum, consisting of two hemispheres. Willis then cut the parts from one another for further study.

By 1663, Willis and his team had completed their research and began creating new brain anatomy diagrams. Willis devised some theories about how the animal spirit moved through the brain and nerves, and he created the term *neurologie*, which meant doctrine of the nerves.

To publish his new book, *The Anatomy of the Brain and Nerves*, Willis had to obtain permission from the church. This book was more than a map of the brain. It basically started what later would be called the science of neurology. Yet he still believed in the earlier, more theologically based ideas about the soul. He still believed that the soul was composed of animal spirits that coursed around the brain and flowed up and down the nervous system. Depending on the size and structure of its brain, a nonhuman animal had animal spirits, as well; these spirits made the different animals move and act in different ways. Yet for humans, the soul had a rational component or sensitivity. This rational soul was not composed of matter. And further, Willis believed that periodically, human souls had to rest by withdrawing into the brain while the person slept.

According to Willis, God put the rational soul into a baby's brain before it was born. The rational soul was immortal and lived beyond the death of the flesh body. Willis went so far as to suggest that the invisible, immortal rational soul dwelled in the corpus callosum, a part of the brain. The sensitive soul, on the other hand, was made of matter and controlled details about everything unrelated to the senses. The rational soul received images and impressions from the sensitive soul and then gave the person ideas, wisdom, decisions, compassion, reason, and will. The rational soul ruled the body. The sensitive soul operated the body and kept all the spirits flowing in an orderly fashion. According to Willis, the two souls fought for power every now and then, and the result was illness inside the brain. For example, the sensitive soul might get tired of being bossed around by the rational soul, and as a result, the sensitive soul might feel sad. The result would be depression. If the sensitive soul became sick enough, even the rational soul was affected; and if the brain was diseased, the rational soul basically went insane: producing delusions and hallucinations. Willis wrote another book to describe his theories about the soul; it was called *Two Discourses Concerning the Soul of Brutes*.

Today, neuroscientists refer to the animal spirits as electrical impulses. Yes, they course through our brains, but they are chemically based neurotransmissions. They pass signals among the neurons, or brain cells.

Neuroscientists are trying to map what happens from neuron to neuron as we see objects and work out math problems. But the idea of consciousness or self remains elusive. Possibly, as I suggested earlier, the soul or self is really a brain-wide synchrony; that is, if we feel happy, it means that complex bunches of neurons are interacting in some way. Consciousness may be part of the physical nature of our individual brains. Not a distinctly different being that controls our brains, but just the collective way our brains function.

PARALLEL WORLDS

Very early in *His Dark Materials*, we learn that other worlds exist. When Lord Asriel first shows his slides, we sense these other realities: "But in the middle of the Aurora, high above the bleak landscape, Lyra could see something solid. . . . [I]n the sky was the unmistakable outline of a city: towers, domes, walls . . . buildings and streets, suspended in the air!" (*The Golden Compass*, page 23).

Soon after this passage, we learn that indeed what Lyra has seen is another world. And later, we're told that there are billions of parallel worlds in *His Dark Materials*.

The Golden Compass is set in Lyra's world, which is somewhat like our world but less advanced. In *The Subtle Knife*, Will's world is very much like our world, yet he quickly steps through a portal into another world that is much different. In this other world, Will and Lyra find a bizarre, ancient Mediterranean city called Cittàgazze, where deadly specters roam and only children survive. After an adventure in the Tower of the Angels, Will and Lyra find Giacomo Paradisi, the bearer of the subtle knife, and soon after, Will loses two fingers in his battle for the knife. Will subsequently uses the subtle knife to open windows into other worlds. The third book, *The Amber Spyglass*, shifts among many parallel worlds, including the afterlife and a weird planet on which creatures ride seedpods.

In simple terms, what are parallel worlds? Is it possible to travel to parallel worlds, and if so, how might this be done? This chapter attempts to answer some of these questions, and along the way, introduces you to current ideas about extraterrestrials, or life on other planets.

Scientists now believe that there may be an infinite number of parallel universes containing "space, time, and other forms of exotic matter."[75] And some of these universes may contain versions of us: That is, you may be sitting in your easy chair right now on planet Earth, reading this book, while another "you" is on another Earthlike planet, flying a helicopter. The other "you" is just like the you on planet Earth, only slightly different. Perhaps the other "you" has a bigger nose, curly hair, and a sharp temper. Or, if the "you" reading this book has a big nose, curly hair, and a sharp temper, then the other "you" might have a tiny nose, straight hair, and a calm demeanor.

According to *Scientific American*, the "simplest and most popular cosmological model today predicts that you have a twin in a galaxy about 10 to the 10^{28} meters from here."[76] Scientists use elementary probability to calculate this estimate; basically, they figure that outer space is infinite and filled with matter in a near-uniform way. Inhabited planets, where extraterrestrials walk, talk, work, and play are everywhere, and our twins, people who are just like us, with the same appearances, the same memories, and even the same names are scattered throughout the galaxies.[77]

---

75. "Parallel Universes." http://www.bbc.co.uk/science/horizon/2001/paralleluni.shtml.
76. Max Tegmark, *Parallel Universes*. www.sciam.com, 2003, p. 41.
77. Ibid.

Today's astronomers can see objects that are approximately 4 × 10^{26} meters away, a distance known as the Hubble volume or more simply as our universe. Each of the infinite parallel universes has its own Hubble volume. About 10 to the 10^{92} meters away is a sphere that has a radius of 100 light years. This sphere is identical to the sphere that is centered here in our universe. Everything that someone sees in that other universe should be the same as everything we see here. Approximately 10 to the 10^{118} meters away is an entire Hubble volume that is identical to the one you're in right now. Further, each universe is part of a gigantic multiverse.

The idea of the multiverse is "grounded in well-tested theories such as relativity and quantum mechanics"[78] and the question is not whether the multiverse exists, but rather, how many levels exist within the multiverse.

Every parallel universe that contains a near-identical you is thought to be a Level 1 multiverse. Oddly enough, the Level 1 multiverse is used routinely by cosmologists.

If we live in a Level 1 multiverse, then it's possible that an infinite number of Level 1 multiverses exist. Each would differ from the others, and collectively, all would be known as a Level 2 multiverse. A theory called chaotic eternal inflation is behind the idea of the Level 2 multiverse.

In 1998, supernova observations reinforced the idea that the universe is expanding. Since then, detailed observations of cosmic background radiation have further confirmed the idea. Scientists believe that space is stretching, hence the use of the word inflation in the theory of chaotic eternal inflation. The accelerating cosmic expansion may be due to the amount of dark energy per cubic centimeter. As discussed in Chapter 2, if scientists knew where dark energy comes from and why it exists in such

78. Ibid.

massive proportions, humans might unlock the secrets behind cosmic expansion. It's been postulated that events in empty space trigger the existence of dark energy. Quantum theory tells us that empty space really isn't "empty"; rather, it consists of virtual particles that "wink in and out of existence so rapidly we can never pin them down directly, but can only observe their effects."[79]

As for the term "chaotic eternal," it refers to what happens when space stops stretching in some spots and forms bubbles until an infinite number of bubbles exist. These bubbles are all different due to the breaking of symmetry. According to one version of this theory, space in our universe once had nine dimensions, but long ago, three of these dimensions evolved during cosmic inflation and became the three dimensions we observe today. This three-dimensional view, or surface, is called a membrane, or brane. The other six dimensions are unobservable, but they do exist. The symmetry that originally existed among the nine dimensions broke when the three observable dimensions split from the other six. Further, the fluctuations that caused chaotic inflation in our universe would cause symmetry breaks in a variety of ways in other universes. The breaks might occur with four observable dimensions, for example.

As recently as December 2004, scientists observed a dozen galaxies that appear as double images, and they believe that their observations form evidence of superstrings, or energy that spans millions of light years throughout the universe. These scientists suggest that the most elemental matter is actually made of these concentrated threads of energy. The vibration of the superstrings varies and is directly related to fundamental particles such as the muon-neutrino; this has become known, actually, as the "theory of everything."[80] Scientists suggest that the only way the superstrings can create all the particles is if they vibrate in a spacetime of ten dimensions.

In simple terms, a dimension is a number that describes a position or motion. To identify the location of an object in space, you use three numbers: latitude, longitude, and altitude. For movement, you can use three directions: forward-backward, up-down, and left-right. Space also has three dimensions, with time being the fourth dimension that creates what we commonly call spacetime.

Physicists today suggest that all of the extra dimensions, the ones we can't see, are extremely tiny. Possibly the extra dimensions are rolled up into tiny objects that are even smaller than an atom. These hidden dimensions may be the keys to the origin of the universe, the existence of dark matter, and the doors to parallel universes.

Some theories about the Big Bang postulate that our universe is a three-dimensional "brane" moving through this superstring ten-dimensional space. Scientists who believe this "brane" theory say that it's possible that the Big Bang occurred when two branes collided.[81] The impact created enormous energy, as well as fundamental superstrings. It's also been postulated that the Big Bang caused what's known as Dirichlet or D branes, which are inside other branes and serve as bridges between the branes. The D branes have only one bridge into one dimension of our universe. However, the theories about D branes and bridges into our universe are only theories: They are not yet proven facts.

In his January 2005 book, *Parallel Worlds*, Michio Kaku writes that scientists today are using high-speed supercomputers, gravity

80. Marcus Chown, "It Came from Another Dimension." *New Scientist*, December 2004, p. 31.
81. *New Scientist*, March 16, 2002, p. 26.

wave detectors, space satellites, lasers, interferometers, and other high-tech instruments to deliver the "most compelling description yet" of the creation of the universe. Indeed, writes Kaku, scientists are now speculating that the biblical Genesis "occurs repeatedly in a timeless ocean of Nirvana" and that "our universe may be compared to a bubble floating in a much larger 'ocean,' with new bubbles forming all the time. According to this theory, universes, like bubbles forming in boiling water, are in continual creation, floating in a much larger arena, the Nirvana of eleven-dimensional hyperspace. A growing number of physicists suggest that our universe did indeed spring forth from a fiery cataclysm, the Big Bang, but that it also coexists in an eternal ocean of other universes."[82]

In addition to theories that predict multiverses far away from us are theories that predict multiverses right in front of our noses. These multiverses are of the type used in *His Dark Materials*. Open a window into another universe that's sitting right in front of you, and *pop*, you're there.

This type of multiverse theory is known as the many worlds interpretation of quantum mechanics; you can think of this theory as the Level 3 quantum many worlds multiverse. Basically, this theory states that random quantum fluctuations occur that cause our universe to branch into infinite multiple copies of itself. For every question you answer, another you could have answered it another way. For every hair on your chin, another you might have the same hair, only a micrometer away.

An entire field of literature has grown out of the idea of quantum many worlds. Parallel universe fiction usually doesn't focus on the events creating the new universes, but rather on

---

82. Michio Kaku, *Parallel Worlds*. New York: Doubleday, January 2005, p. 5. Kaku is the Henry Semat Professor of Theoretical Physics at the Graduate Center of the City University of New York. He's the author of many famous books and articles about hyperspace and parallel worlds.

what happens after the new universes exist. For example, popular stories center on what the world would have been like if the South had won the Civil War or what the world would be like now if the American Revolution had failed and the United States was still a British colony. While not all parallel world stories deal with wars, the concept is popular with military science fiction writers because wars usually have key moments when a decision one way or another will have a profound effect on the future.[83] In Ward Moore's parallel world novel, *Bring the Jubilee*, the main character travels back in time to change history by making sure the South doesn't win the Civil War. In Ray Bradbury's classic story, "A Sound of Thunder," a man who time-travels back to the age of dinosaurs changes modern history by accidentally stepping on a butterfly millions of years in the past.

Even if we consider the major events in history as moments when the universe branches into two new realities, the number is staggering. How many major events have occurred in human history? Thousands, tens of thousands, hundreds of thousands, millions? Plus, every time a new reality is created, events in its future will also result in parallel worlds. And this branching effect has been going on since the beginning of history. So the number of branches is in the billions of billions.[84]

As Ray Bradbury demonstrated, even the smallest change in the Jurassic Age could have changed all the history that came afterward. Even the first volcanic eruption on the newly formed Earth might have affected the air we breathe today. Every event that has ever happened must be analyzed when determining how many parallel worlds might exist and what they're like. The num-

---

83. I take the liberty of quoting myself extensively here. For complete details, see the extensive chapter on infinite worlds in: Lois H. Gresh and Robert Weinberg, "Crisis on Infinite Earths" in *The Science of Supervillains*. New York: John Wiley & Sons, Inc., 2004, pp. 143–157.
84. Ibid.

ber of parallel universes that exist in direct relationship to our own world is a function of the number of events that have taken place since the creation of Earth.[85]

The many worlds interpretation was first proposed by Hugh Everett III when he was a Princeton graduate student in 1957. According to Everett's theory, whenever multiple possibilities exist in quantum events, the world splits into many worlds, one for each possibility. These worlds are all real and exist simultaneously with the first, while remaining unobservable by any of the others.

Everett's theory is not well liked by many physicists who prefer the Copenhagen Interpretation of Quantum Mechanics, developed by Niels Bohr and Werner Heisenberg in the late 1920s (in Copenhagen). The Copenhagen interpretation says that in quantum mechanics, measurement outcomes are basically indeterministic. Albert Einstein was a strong opponent of the Copenhagen interpretation, expressing his doubts in the famous line, "God does not play dice."[86]

While the Copenhagen Interpretation of Quantum Mechanics is fascinating, we'll stick with the more interesting many worlds theory. Working with that concept, we find that the number of alternate universes for the Earth, while incredibly large, is finite. Since the Earth has not existed forever, if we had a gigantic computer and a lot of spare time for calculating, we could come up with the number of all possible quantum events that have taken place since the Earth was formed. We could thus calculate every possible parallel universe created by those events. From there, we could track down every possible quantum event that took place in all these branch universes. Continuing outward, following every possible branch, counting quantum events

85. Ibid.
86. http://www.nationmaster.com/encyclopedia/Copenhagen-interpretation.

at the speed of light, we could record billions upon billions of probability worlds that are linked to the first quantum action on the planet Earth. The number would be mind-boggling. Still, the sum of an immense but finite group of immense finite numbers is a finite number. So, though the voyage would be staggering, since the number of universes created by the Earth over its billions of years of history is finite, we could travel from the first created parallel universe to the last. Science fiction stories that discuss the details of traveling across millions upon millions of parallel universes include work by Poul Anderson, Andre Norton, H. Beam Piper, and Keith Laumer.

But is that immensely huge number the total of all parallel universes that exist? We've dealt with the many worlds theory as it relates only to the Earth. However, the Earth is just one planet, part of one solar system, part of one galaxy, part of one galaxy cluster, part of our universe. Since the entire universe contains atoms whose particles are subject to the laws of quantum mechanics, every atom in the universe is subject to the many worlds theory. While the life cycle of planets, stars, and even galaxies is finite, our current theory about the universe states that it began with a Big Bang billions of years ago and has been expanding ever since, creating new stars, new solar systems, and new galaxies as it does. As we understand it, the universe is infinite in size. Thus, we have an infinite number of atomic particles whose movement creates parallel universes throughout the entire universe. In other words, since there are an infinite number of atomic particles, there are an infinite number of parallel universes.

The many worlds interpretation also ranges back to the Schrödinger equation. Erwin Schrödinger was an Austrian physicist who lived from 1887 to 1961, and he was a pioneer of quantum physics. He devised a famous, yet imaginary, experiment involving a cat.

Schrödinger noted that when an atom decays, there might be

a one in ten chance that it will decay in thirty minutes, a nine in ten chance that it will decay within one day, and so forth. Further, if you're observing the atom at a particular moment, it's either decaying or it isn't decaying; at that moment, there is a fifty-fifty chance that the atom is decaying. The atom is in a "confused" state, not knowing whether to decay or not decay within that particular moment. Now what if you're not watching the atom?

Schrödinger suggested that, in an imaginary experiment, we might put a "confused" radioactive atom in a locked box with a living cat. The atom alone could not hurt the cat, but if the decay of the atom triggered a killing device, then should the atom decay, the poor cat would be killed. When the atom is in the fifty-fifty state, is the cat dead or alive?

The Copenhagen Interpretation mandates that nothing is real unless you look at it. So if you open the box and look at the cat, you'll know whether it's dead or alive. However, if nobody opens the door and looks at the cat, then there's no way to know whether the cat is dead or alive during the moment when the atom is in its fifty-fifty "confused" state. You could say that the cat is dead and alive at the same time.

In terms of the many worlds interpretation, what Schrödinger's cat theory tells us is that all the parallel universes are real, even though we can't see them. The cat is both dead and alive at the same time: According to the many worlds interpretation, in one world, the cat is alive, and in another world, the cat is dead. If you exist in this world, open the box, and see a live cat, then another you in another world is opening the box and seeing a dead cat.

And each time anything in the quantum realm has a choice—to decay or not decay, for example—the universe splits in this way. All of these parallel universes exist simultaneously.

The multiverse theory suggests that different laws of nature might exist on infinite worlds. It also suggests that life might exist—in fact, probably does exist—on many other worlds. As *National Geographic* points out in its lead article for December 2004, "Astronomers are more certain than ever that other planets like our own exist in the universe. Now they just have to find them."[87] And as Michio Kaku wrote in January 2005, "Physicists and astronomers around the world are now speculating about what these parallel worlds may look like, what laws they might obey, how they are born, and how they may eventually die. . . . Perhaps they look just like our universe, separated by a single quantum event that made these universes diverge from ours. . . . The engine driving these new theories is the massive flood of data that is pouring from our space satellites as they photograph remnants of creation itself."[88]

The concept that we are not alone in the universe isn't new. It's a subject that's been examined by philosophers, as well as scientists, for thousands of years. *Pluralism* is defined as the belief that the universe is filled with planets harboring intelligent life.[89]

Pluralism was first championed by the Greek atomist philosophers Leucippus, Democritus of Abdera, and Epicurus in the fifth century B.C. These men believed that the Earth was the product of a chance collision of indestructible particles known as atoms. Since one world had been formed in such a fashion, they argued that other worlds with intelligent life were possible as well. Opposing the atomists were Aristotle and Plato, who argued that the Earth was unique and that no other worlds or intelligent life-forms existed.

Needless to say, the Aristotelian view of the universe was accepted by the Catholic Church because that viewpoint gave

87. Tim Appenzeller, "Someplace Like Earth." *National Geographic*, December 2004, p. 68.
88. Michio Kaku, op. cit., pp. 5–6.
89. Here I take the liberty of quoting myself extensively from: Lois Gresh and Robert Weinberg, *The Science of Superheroes*. New York: John Wiley & Sons, 2002, pp. 4–14.

man a special place in the universe. However, in the late twelfth century, a number of scholars raised some serious religious arguments against Aristotle's belief that there was only one possible cosmos. Since God was omnipotent, these men declared, then stating God created only one universe was in a sense placing restrictions on God's power, which would thus imply that God was not all-powerful. In 1277, the church eased its stance on the unique nature of the universe. Catholic doctrine was revised to say that God *could* have created other worlds with intelligent beings, but hadn't.

It was a very small step for science but a major one. Following the same line of reasoning, Nicholas of Cusa in 1440 declared that whatever God could do, would be done, a belief that became known as *plenitude*. Less than a century later, Copernicus argued convincingly that the sun was the center of the solar system and the Earth was merely a planet revolving about it. Copernicus wisely didn't delve into the theological ramifications of his discovery, but other scholars and philosophers were soon debating the possibility of life on other worlds.

For the next several hundred years, proponents and opponents of plenitude and pluralism argued about God's purpose in creating a universe filled with stars and planets. As usual, in debates where men tried to explain God's purpose, neither side convinced the other that they were correct. Fortunately, by the mid-nineteenth century, developments in science and astronomy made such debates moot. God's intent faded in the face of the theory of evolution, and a scientific view of the universe slowly but surely replaced the religious one.

Still, while pluralism and plenitude were interesting theories, there was no factual evidence to back up either philosophy. There were numerous theories about life on other planets, but there was no proof. Telescopes could show only so much. There were no canals on Mars, and the clouds of Venus didn't shroud gigantic oceans or primeval forests. The only aliens from other worlds appeared in science fiction books and magazines.

World War II left the American public cynical and disillusioned. The atomic bomb displayed the frightening power of new technology. The Yalta Conference, concentration camps, and the Berlin blockade pushed distrust of politicians to an all-time high. Nuclear power plant stories filled newspaper Sunday supplements. Space travel seemed only a few years away. After years of stories about life on other planets, people started wondering where the aliens were and whether it was possible that we were the most intelligent species in the universe. If the galaxy was so huge and full of life, why hadn't other life-forms contacted us?

As always when a question's raised, someone was there with an answer. It's not surprising that the average citizen, living in a Cold War atmosphere of distrust and misinformation, was more than willing to believe that our government was concealing the truth about aliens from other planets. In 1947, we suddenly "learned" from several "nonfiction" books and magazine articles that other eyes were watching. It was the beginning of the flying saucer craze. Flying saucers became part of our vocabulary. They were featured in innumerable magazine stories and tell-all books, and they dominated late-night talk radio. Saucers have remained in our skies for the past half century despite the lack of any conclusive evidence proving their existence. In 2001, surveys indicated that a majority of people in this country believe Earth has been visited by aliens.

Suddenly, the question wasn't whether aliens existed on other planets. Instead, the question became: Why are the aliens spying on us?

Flying saucers were a major setback for scientists trying to prove that extraterrestrial life existed in the galaxy. Frank Drake, one of the leading astronomers of the twentieth century, put it best when he stated that pseudo-science leads to false "knowledge," which leads to wrong decisions, wrong choices of technologies, a wrong distribution of resources, wrong priorities, wrong choice of leaders. Thus, the unfortunate result of the widespread public confusion as to the relative promise of pseudo-scientific studies of UFOs . . . as compared with true scientific programs to find life on other planets is that less attention is given to the "real science" than to the pseudo-science.[90]

So whether you believe in flying saucers or think that they're an ongoing money-making hoax, where are the aliens? If they're here, why are they so shy? After all, building a ship that can navigate the far reaches of outer space takes a fairly sophisticated and advanced civilization—one a good deal more advanced than ours. They can't all be tongue-tied or hiding under sofa cushions. Surely one of them has something to say to the world at large. Even a quick "Hi" would satisfy most people.

Imagine the worldwide excitement there would be if a flying saucer landed on the White House lawn and a humanoid figure stepped out to bring greetings from another planet. A visit like that would change the world overnight. We'd actually know that we aren't alone in the universe; not to mention that we aren't the smartest or even the strongest kids in the neighborhood.

Pluralism and plenitude are interesting theories but have no basis in fact. Are there alien civilizations in the galaxy? Do we have any proof at all that we are not alone in the universe other than religious doctrine?

In the 1950s, astronomer Frank Drake (quoted above) proposed an equation to estimate the number of intelligent species in our galaxy, the Milky Way. This equation served as the rallying point for the earliest efforts to use radio telescopes to detect signals sent by other highly advanced civilizations. Run for months by

90. Frank Drake, foreword to *Sharing the Universe*, by Seth Shostak. Berkeley, CA: Berkeley Hills Books, 1998, pp. i–ii.

Drake, Project Ozma had no success in detecting the all-important radio signals from other star systems. However, a far greater effort was organized by scientists and continues to this day. The Search for Extraterrestrial Intelligence (SETI) served as the background for Carl Sagan's book (later made into a movie) *Contact*.

The Drake Equation is a fairly simple multiplication problem.

$$N = R^* \times f_p \times ne \times f_t \times f_i \times f_c \times L$$

where

N is the number of intelligent civilizations in the galaxy (the number we are looking for).

R^* is the birthrate of suitable stars for life in the Milky Way galaxy measured in stars per year.

f_p is the fraction of stars with planets.

ne is the number of planets in a star's habitable zone (which we define below).

f_t is the percentage of civilizations that have the technology and desire to communicate with other worlds.

f_i is the fraction of habitable planets where life does arise.

f_c is the fraction of planets inhabited by intelligent beings.

L is the average in years of how long technologically advanced civilizations last. In other words, how long is it from the time aliens invent radios to when their civilization either destroys itself or disappears?

The only phrase that's confusing is a "star's habitable zone." In simplest terms, the phrase refers to the imaginary shell around a star where the surface temperature of a planet in that shell would be conducive to the origin and development of life. As far as humanity is concerned, the habitable zone around a star is the space where planets exist that have water in liquid form, the most basic necessity for life. In our solar system, Earth is obviously in the Habitable Zone. Venus, which is too close to the sun, is not. Nor is Mars, which is too far away.

In the 1950s, when Frank Drake invented the Drake Equation, many of the numbers and fractions were not known. As our knowledge of astronomy grew, more of the numbers became available. Still, some were based more on hopes and beliefs than actual information.

A very popular theory about the universe believed by Carl Sagan and other space scientists is known as the Principle of Mediocrity (sometimes called the Copernican Principle). This theory, based entirely on logic, states that since Earth appears to be a quite typical and common planet, intelligence has a very high probability of emerging on any planet similar to Earth after 3.5 billion years of evolution.

In simplest terms, the Principle of Mediocrity states that Earth isn't special, so there should be lots of other planets with life on them.

Belief in the Principle of Mediocrity fuels the scientists who believe in SETI. It's also what makes the Drake Equation work. Without it, we'd most likely not have stories about the *mulefa* and visitors in flying saucers. However, in the past decade, a growing number of scientists have been studying the Principle of Mediocrity, and they find it wanting. We'll discuss this idea in a minute.

For the moment, let's plug some numbers into the Drake Equation. To put things in perspective, let's use the numbers that Frank Drake and Carl Sagan used and see how many intelligent extraterrestrial civilizations are out there.

R^* has been estimated by astronomers to be between one and ten stars per year. Drake picked five as an average.

For f_p, the number of stars with planets, Sagan believed that a majority of stars had planets. In the past few years, we've actually located some. Let's be somewhat conservative and pick twenty percent, or one out of every five stars.

For ne, the number of planets that exist in the habitable

zone, if we use our solar system as a model (the Principle of Mediocrity), then the number is one.

For f_l, the percentage of worlds like Earth where life begins, Drake and Sagan chose one hundred percent, again using Earth as their model.

For f_c, the percentage of planets with intelligent life, SETI scientists argue that evolution over billions of years leads to intelligence, so again the percentage could also be one hundred percent.

For f_t, intelligent species who develop the technology and the desire to communicate with other worlds, Drake estimates that this value is one hundred percent.

The math is pretty basic. Multiply all the numbers we have so far and (surprise, surprise) we end up with an equation that $N = L$. This is the same result that Frank Drake and Carl Sagan arrived at years ago: The number of intelligent civilizations in the galaxy equals the average lifetime of technologically advanced civilizations.

Again, let's assume that Earth is average (using the Principle of Mediocrity). If our civilization self-destructed next year due to terrorism or the release of a deadly plague virus, then L would be approximately 100, meaning that our galaxy would be home to one hundred alien civilizations. Considering that there are somewhere between 200 and 400 billion stars in our galaxy, we suddenly are faced with the possibility of one civilization per two billion to four billion stars. It's no wonder we haven't been contacted by aliens. Reducing it to more human terms, it would be as if two people were born on the Earth during the past fifty years, separated not only by time but by thousands of miles. Neither has any clue about the other except that they have the same birthmarks. Then somehow, they must find each other, searching on foot.

Frank Drake and Carl Sagan both knew that L, the lifetime of a technologically advanced civilization, was the great stumbling block in the Drake Equation. However, both men were not only scientists but optimists. Drake felt that a technological civilization might last for ten thousand years. Thus, he estimated that there were ten thousand advanced civilizations in the galaxy.[91] This would leave us with one civilization per twenty to forty million stars, still somewhat of a daunting search. Other scientists believe that number to be much too low. They estimate that there could be hundreds of thousands of such civilizations. Which would mean we're not as alone as we thought.

More important to our concerns, the Drake Equation, working with the figures cited, gives us estimates ranging from 100 to 10,000 civilizations in the galaxy.

Our home galaxy, the Milky Way, is only 100,000 light years across. There are approximately twenty other galaxies, some much larger than the Milky Way and some much smaller, within three million light years, increasing our range of possible civilizations from 2,000 to 200,000.

Even if there are only a few hundred civilizations per galaxy, there are a lot of galaxies in the known universe. A recent estimate placed the number at fifty billion galaxies. Assuming one hundred civilizations per galaxy, that still results in five thousand billion (5,000,000,000,000) intelligent civilizations in the known universe. If we take Frank Drake's more optimistic guess, we're talking about 500,000,000,000,000 (five hundred trillion!) advanced civilizations in the universe.

But don't tell Peter D. Ward and Donald Brownlee that. Because they've raised some serious doubts about the Drake Equation.

---

91. Carl Sagan, who was even more of an optimist than Drake, estimated in 1974 that there might be a million civilized planets in our galaxy.

In their 2000 book, *Rare Earth: Why Complex Life Is Uncommon in the Universe*, Ward and Brownlee discuss the Principle of Mediocrity. The two scientists argue that perhaps we've gone too far in trying to prove that man isn't special. They argue that in our attempts to understand the universe surrounding us, we've downsized the significance of life on Earth. Perhaps, they propose, life is not common and the Principle of Mediocrity isn't true. Maybe, as the ancient religious thinkers believe, mankind is unique.

It's a startling proposition, but the two men build a compelling case. Chapter by chapter, they examine each factor in Frank Drake's famous equation and arrive at totally different conclusions.

The basic problem with the Drake Equation is that it's a series of numbers multiplied together that give us a final answer. In any multiplication problem, if any one number is zero, the answer is zero. If any one number is a very small fraction, the answer becomes a small fraction. If the assumptions used to produce those numbers are incorrect, then the numbers are invalid. In the Drake Equation, too many of the numbers are based entirely on speculation, hope, and faith, not on fact.

Let's examine four of the most troubling figures in the Drake Equation. Instead of taking the optimistic viewpoint adopted by the people working on SETI, let's instead look at them with a much more pessimistic eye, the viewpoint of *Rare Earth*.

For example, f_p is the fraction of stars with planets. Our solar system has nine planets. Carl Sagan argued that an average solar system most likely would have ten or more. Other noted scientists of the 1970s and 1980s felt that ten planets was a good estimate. However, major strides in astronomy during the past decades have caused astronomers to rethink this belief.

In the last ten years, scientists have discovered twenty-seven planetary bodies circling other stars. All of the planets we've located are huge, about the size of Jupiter, the largest planet in our solar system. Astronomers studied numerous stars to find the twenty-seven stars with huge planets circling them. No method has yet been developed to locate smaller, Earth-sized planets. So, the guess that f_p is one of every five stars with planets could be extremely high. We probably won't have a good estimate on the average until we start traveling to other solar systems.

Ne is the number of planets in a star's habitable zone. Until recently, the Habitable Zone has been defined as the appropriate distance from a star that enables liquid water to exist and complex life to develop. Earth is the only planet in the Habitable Zone of our solar system. It's possible that some sort of simple biological life might exist or once have existed on Mars, but that hasn't been proven.

Ward and Brownlee argue in their book that based on what we've learned about astronomy in the past few decades, it's clear that Habitable Zones are a lot more complicated than anything imagined by Drake and Sagan in the 1960s or 1970s. For example, they point out that the presence of Jupiter, a massive gas giant much farther out in our solar system, was a critical factor in life developing on Earth. Jupiter's immense gravitational pull attracted most comets to it instead of allowing them to crash into Earth. Without a Jupiter-sized planet serving as this type of shield against stray comets, life on Earth would have been subject to mass extinction events and planetary disasters caused by space collisions.

Therefore, the Habitable Zone of a solar system isn't merely based on the location of a planet in a solar system, but on the location of other planets in the system as well. Which makes the existence of Habitable Zones a great deal less probable than was once considered.

Ward and Brownlee take Habitable Zones a step farther by considering the zone of space where animal life, not merely biological life, could develop. Biological life, such as primitive bacteria, can exist in extreme heat or extreme cold. Humans can't and the difference needs to be taken into account.

F_i is the fraction of habitable planets where life does arise. In *Rare Earth*, the authors examine the length of time, measured in billions of years, necessary for a Habitable Zone to exist in relative stability for evolution to take place. Using Earth as our model, that time zone needs to be at least three billion years long. They point out that our sun, a G2 type star, has a lifetime of ten billion years, more than enough time for complex life to develop.

However, G2 suns are not the most common stars in the galaxy. That honor belongs to M stars, which have a mass of only about ten percent of our sun. As these stars don't emit nearly as much heat as Sol, the Habitable Zone around them is much closer to the star itself. Planets would need to orbit much nearer to the sun, which leads to a host of problems. Gravitational tidal effects from the star can lock the planet into an orbit where only one side of the planet faces the sun—an orbit like that of Mercury. It's an orbit that's not conducive to life.

Going in the other direction, stars more massive than our sun have a much shorter lifetime. Sol is predicted to remain stable for ten billion years. A star fifty percent more massive than our sun would last only two billion years before entering the red giant stage. When a regular star transforms into a red giant, all planets in the original Habitable Zone in space are burned away, as new Habitable Zones are established millions of miles further out.

Big hot stars like Sirius also generate a lot of their energy as ultraviolet light. UV light is fatal to biological molecules, so any star system with a high density sun wouldn't be the home of carbon-based beings. So f_i might be a complex problem, involving Habitable Zones, the structure of the solar system, and the type of suns at the center of the same system.

The situation becomes murkier and definitely not better. F_c

is the fraction of planets on which life develops intelligence. Frank Drake felt that every place where life began, intelligent life would arise. That's an optimistic viewpoint, based entirely on the fact that intelligent life developed on Earth. The more we learn about the slow, complex path of evolution from single-celled organisms to a walking, talking, thinking man, the less sure that number becomes. Drake and Sagan argued that intelligence was inevitable on any planet where life began. Many scientists now believe that considering the more than three billion years it took for complex, intelligent life to evolve on Earth, we were very lucky.

If we could compress time so that one second equaled ten thousand years, all of humanity's recorded history could be squeezed into one second. Mankind's rise from simple predator to ruler of the Earth fills three seconds. However, the time it took for one-celled organisms to evolve into intelligent life spans two and a half days. During that long slow rise, paleontologists know of at least ten extinction level events where more than half of all known life on Earth was destroyed. Optimists would argue that the development of intelligent life on Earth despite these ten extinction level events demonstrates that complex life is inevitable. Pessimists would argue that we've been fortunate and the next extinction level event could be our last one.

If f_c is less than one hundred percent, then what of f_t, the number of alien races who will try to communicate with other species from another planet? Frank Drake and the scientists of SETI believe that percentage to be one hundred percent—that every race of beings in the universe wants to discover intelligent life elsewhere. They base their assumption on *our* behavior. But aliens, being alien, probably will have little or nothing in common with us. They might not be curious, or a vast number of them might not want to use their resources to contact other races in space. Instead, they may spend their money on the poor, the homeless, and the hungry. F_t could be one hundred percent, but it just as likely could be one percent. If the Drake Equation is to have any relevance, we need to consider both possibilities.

If we plug all the worst-case scenario numbers into the Drake Equation, then estimate that L is 1,000 rather than 10,000, the result is that there may be only one civilization in the Milky Way galaxy. Like it or not, we may actually be alone in our galaxy.

Of course, that doesn't mean that we're alone in the universe, or more significantly, in the multiverse. In 2000, David Darling wrote, "Poised on the brink of a momentous breakthrough that will change forever how humankind thinks about itself and the universe around it, astrobiology is quickly coming of age."[92] And further: "Almost beyond doubt, life exists elsewhere."[93]

Astrobiology is the latest buzzword among scientists who believe that life exists on other planets. They point to microbes that have been discovered on what we once thought were areas of our own planet that were incapable of supporting life. For example, we now know that microorganisms thrive in scorching underground rocks, in volcanic vents deep beneath the sea, and in the Arctic ice cap. We've found evidence of life on other planets, such as Mars. It's now thought by many scientists that life can indeed thrive in alien environments.

While astrobiology has been known by other names, such as exobiology, it was embraced as a science in 1998 when NASA created the NASA Astrobiology Institute. The budget was small, only five million dollars in 1998; and rose only to fifteen million

92. David Darling, *Life Everywhere: The Maverick Science of Astrobiology*. New York: Basic Books, 2001, p. xiii.
93. Ibid., p. xi.

in 2002. Recently, two new journals have popped up on the scene: *Astrobiology* and the *International Journal of Astrobiology*. In addition, astrobiology centers are now in many parts of the world, including Japan, France, England, Australia, and Spain.

Physicist Michio Kaku told *Astrobiology Magazine* in 2004 that the question of whether there are billions of habitable worlds available for evolving complex life "is no longer a matter of idle speculation." Noting that every few weeks brought "news of a new Jupiter-sized extra-solar planet being discovered"—the latest then being about fifteen light years away, orbiting around the star Gliese 876—Kaku predicted that humanity may soon face an existential shock as the current list of a dozen Jupiter-sized extra-solar planets swells to hundreds of Earth-sized planets, almost identical twins of our celestial homeland. Within ten years, we'll be launching the Space Interferometry Mission, which will house many telescopes on a thirty-foot structure. In the next decade, we'll launch the Terrestial Planet Finder, which will "scan the brightest 1,000 stars within 50 light years of Earth."[94]

The search is on. . . .

94. An interview with Michio Kaku in *Astrobiology Magazine*, April 26, 2004, as reported at http://www.astrobio.net/news.

THE AFTERLIFE: HELL, HARPIES, AND HEAVEN

Philip Pullman introduces us to his world of the dead in the third novel of *His Dark Materials*. It's in *The Amber Spyglass* that we encounter the ghosts of all dead people and the land of no return, where death prevails over a bleak landscape. The world of the dead is also called the land of the dead interchangeably in *His Dark Materials*.

As soon as we open *The Amber Spyglass*, Roger is calling to Lyra from the world of the dead, which is described as a vast plain of bare earth with no light, a black sky, and mist everywhere. When a person dies, his body is gone forever, his daemon dies with it, but his ghost lives on in the world of the dead. "This was the end of all places and the last of all worlds" (*The Amber Spyglass*, opening).

Later, the angel Balthamos explains that the world of the dead is a prison camp created by the Authority long ago. Baruch adds that the countless millions of people, kings and paupers alike, are in the world of the dead as ghosts, but that, fortunately, Balthamos spared the ghost of Baruch such eternal misery. So apparently not all ghosts of dead people dwell in the world of the dead: Angels are able to pardon the ghosts of some.

Later, Will and Lyra discuss how to get into the world of the dead to find Roger and save him. Lyra determines that Will can use the subtle knife to carve a window into the world of the dead. But the two children worry about their daemons, or souls, which fade away when people die. What will happen to Lyra's daemon if she enters the world of the dead? Yet the alethiometer tells her that she and Will must go there and rescue Roger, so they decide to take their chances.

After a long trek, Will, Lyra, and the two Gallivespians, Tialys and Salmakia, come to a village, which they think is the world of the dead. Everywhere are the ghosts of people who have just died. "The edges of things were losing their definition and becoming blurred. The color was slowly seeping out of the world" (*The Amber Spyglass*, page 248). The ghosts in the village are afraid of Will and Lyra. They're not at all fearsome like the ghosts we think of in our own reality. Instead, these ghosts are stumbling, unaware of their destination but dragging behind one another in an endless trail toward . . . something.

Following the endless trail of frightened ghosts, Will, Lyra, Tialys, and Salmakia arrive at an ancient refugee camp that borders a vast lake covered in mist. By the time they reach the camp, the ghosts are in trances, much like zombies. A man tells Will and Lyra that they must leave immediately, that this place is only for the dead; it is a port of transit for the ghosts, who will travel to the world of the dead by boat (*The Amber Spyglass*, pages 250–254).

These ghosts in the world of the dead are not the same as the specters that eat people in the world of Cittàgazze. Rather, these ghosts are distinct beings that are with people throughout life. A living person can even talk to his death, as Lyra does: "The death stood very close, smiling kindly, his face exactly like those of all the others she'd seen; but this was hers, her very own death . . ." (*The Amber Spyglass*, page 266). Oddly, Lyra's death is male, as is her soul.

It is Lyra's death who explains that when she dies, her body will be buried, her soul will simply vanish, and her ghost will go to the world of the dead. Lyra persuades her death to act as a guide into the world of the dead so she can find Roger.

To gain access to the world of the dead, Lyra must leave her daemon behind in the refugee camp. Souls are not allowed in the afterworld. She and Will climb into the rowboat for the trip across the lake to an island that serves as the gateway into the world of the dead.

Here they encounter the harpies: giant birds that look like vultures with the faces and breasts of human females. The harpies have lived for thousands of years, filled with hatred and cruelty, with eye sockets "clotted with filthy slime" and with lips "caked and crusted as if [they] had vomited ancient blood again and again" (*The Amber Spyglass*, page 289). The guardian of the gate is a harpy with jagged claws, dark wings, and a smell like death. The harpy shrieks, jeers at the children, and tries to make them feel like wretched human beings. For example, the harpy tells Will that all the harpies will give his poor mother terrible nightmares and shriek so she cannot sleep (*The Amber Spyglass*, pages 290–291).

Eventually, Will and Lyra enter the world of the dead, where they find Roger. They convince the harpies to help them (in exchange for the telling of good stories), and the harpies lead the children to a window leading from the world of the dead. From there, Will and Lyra lead all the ghosts, including Roger, from the world of the dead up through a cave, where the ghosts float apart with great glee and dissipate into the vastness of the universe.

The world of the dead isn't hell. The world of the dead isn't heaven. It's a place where the ghosts of all dead people come (*The Amber Spyglass*, page 320).

It's interesting to note that people all over the world, regardless of religion and ethnic background, believe in some form of life after death. Most humans think that a part of us—the soul, the personality, the spirit—exists beyond the grave. Ideas about the way this happens and the part of us that survives death differ from culture to culture.

Some cultures believe that the dead influence our lives and make special requests on our behalf to the gods. Some cultures believe that the dead appear to us as ghosts to help or harm us. And we, in turn, offer prayers to the dead to keep them happy with us, to aid them in the afterlife, and to avoid any harm they might cast upon us.

Many cultures also believe in a world of the dead, where our spirits, souls, or personalities (ghosts, perhaps?) dwell forever in a gloomy, bleak prisonlike place; Ananka and Sheol, which we'll discuss in a minute, are examples of these types of worlds of the dead, very similar to the one painted in *His Dark Materials*. Yet there are many other cultures who believe in worlds of the dead that are happy and sunny, that are sprawling and full of regions similar to those on Earth. Some examples of these worlds of the dead might be Valhalla and Tir na n-Og.

Of course, the worlds of the dead usually include some notion of purgatory—where we go en route to heaven and hell, so judges can determine our ultimate destinations—as well as the final resting places of heaven for good people, hell for those who have sinned. Most cultures include rivers, lakes, or other bodies of water in their myths about the afterlife; and boatmen, bridges, guardians, and gates are common as well. This chapter explores these and other topics within the overall context of *His Dark Materials*.

In ancient times, people all over the world believed that life existed after death. The Sumerians, who lived near the Persian Gulf in Iraq, wrote about the land of the dead four thousand years ago. Their descriptions were on baked clay tablets. The Sumerians, the Akkadians who conquered them, the Babylonians, and the Assyrians are generally known as the Mesopotamians, and they shared many beliefs, including ideas about the afterlife.

Included in the Mesopotamian view of the afterlife are a river, boatmen, guardians, and gates. The most famous Mesopotamian afterlife story is *Gilgamesh*, which takes place in the actual world of the dead.

Led by the Sky God, the Mesopotamian gods live in the Great Above. The Queen of Heaven and Earth is known as Inanna by the Sumerians, Ishtar by the Akkadians, Astarte by the Assyrians, and Asthoreth by the Canaanites. In the Great Below in the Land of No Return, where the dead reside, Queen Ereshkigal rules. The Earthly Paradise is on the Isle of the Blest beyond the Mountains of Mashu and serves as an Eden to one human male and his wife.

Also prevalent all over the world is the notion of hell. In most cultures, a brave hero or heroine travels into the land of the dead to bring someone back or perform some other amazing feat. The earliest tale of this type is also from ancient Sumeria.

In the story, Inanna, the Queen of Heaven and Earth, wants to visit her sister, Ereshkigal, Queen of the Great Below in the Land of No Return. She dons her finest clothes and priceless jewels, and she sets off on her journey. At the first lapis lazuli gate into the world of the dead, Inanna is stopped by a guardian of the gate. Note the similarity between this ancient Sumerian story and *The Amber Spyglass*. Will and Lyra are also stopped by a guardian, the harpy, at a gate into the world of the dead.

As the story continues, Inanna makes it from one gate to another, and at each, a guardian removes some of her clothing and jewels until, at last, when she reaches the seventh and final gate, she is completed naked. Luckily for Lyra, there is only one gate, and the only thing taken from her is her soul. Finally, Ereshkigal appears, and being thoroughly ticked off at her sister for putting her through such "hell," Inanna leaps at her sister in anger. Ereshkigal releases sixty miseries upon poor Inanna; and in other versions of the story, hangs Inanna on a stake. We could pause and comment here on the dysfunctional family of today and how it just doesn't compare to the dysfunctional family of Sumeria, but we'll continue with our story. . . .

Eventually, Inanna's friend in the world of the living begs the gods for her release. And the lovely sister, Ereshkigal, finally lets Inanna leave the world of the dead. But only if Inanna sends a re-placement to dwell in the world of the dead. Ereshkigal sends a bunch of nasty goblins into the world of the living to make sure Inanna casts a poor human into the world of the dead, and be-cause a lover boy named Dumuzi was having fun during her ab-sence, Inanna casts him into eternal misery. They strike a bargain, and Dumuzi ends up spending half the year in the world of the dead and Dumuzi's sister ends up spending the other half of the year there.

So much for a friendly visit to one's sister. . . .

In the *Gilgamesh* tale, the king of Uruk, whose name hap-pens to be Gilgamesh, and his friend Enkidu offend Inanna. The gods decide that either Gilgamesh or Enkidu must die. Enkidu has a terrible nightmare, in which he dies; and Gilgamesh sets off to find the land of the dead and its immortal inhabitant, Ziusudra. Gilgamesh travels through darkness, a place of no color, through the Mountains of Mashu. From there, he comes to the sea, where a boatman tells him that his journey is absurd and hopeless. Again, we notice the similarity between the Gilgamesh story and that of *His Dark Materials*, in which the boatman reluc-tantly agrees to ferry Lyra, Will, and their friends into the land of the dead. Gilgamesh hops onto the boat and makes his way to an

enchanted island, just as Lyra and Will make their way to the island in *The Amber Spyglass*.

Just as the ancient Sumerians left us a book of the dead—or
rather, clay tablets of the dead—the ancient Egyptians left us a
book of the dead. In the case of the Egyptians, the book of the
dead was written on papyrus thousands of years ago and included all sorts of spells enabling the dead to have safe journeys
through the underworld.

During the Old Kingdom of Egypt, approximately 2200 B.C.,
the Egyptian nobility were the only ones who lived after death.
During the Middle Kingdom, approximately 1570 B.C., the Egyptians wrote of Osiris, their god of the dead, who also served as the
judge of those entering his kingdom. Like the Christian Jesus,
Osiris was a form of sacrificed and resurrected godhead; and
Osiris's son, Horus, was god of all the living.

Upon death, the Egyptian life force, called the *ka*, and the
Egyptian soul, called the *ba*, left the dead body. The *ka* and the
ba (which looked like a bird with a human head) traveled on a
boat over the river of the sky. The *ka* and *ba* then made their way
through seven gates, and at each gate had to please a gatekeeper,
a watcher, and a herald. In a Hall of Justice in the house of
Osiris, the *ka* and *ba* received white garments and sandals to
wear. Thoth, the god of wisdom, tried to prosecute the dead person for crimes committed during life, and finally, the judge Osiris
put the dead person's heart on a scale of justice. He weighed the
heart against a feather given to him by Maat, the goddess of
truth. If the heart sank lower on its scale than Maat's feather,
then a monster called Ammit ate the heart, and the person was
not granted entry into the afterlife.

If indeed the heart weighed less than the feather, meaning
that the dead person had led a moral and decent life, then Osiris
allowed the dead person's life force and soul into the world of the

dead. Here, the dead person was somewhat resurrected in a new body clad in the white garment and sandals. Here, he continued to use the book of the dead, which contained spells to protect him from monsters, suffocation, and even from dying again. At this point, the dead person tried to transform himself into another form, such as a bird, a flower, or a snake. This new form would correspond somewhat to the dead person's personality: Notice the similarity here to the concept in *His Dark Materials* that a soul, or daemon, takes a physical form that represents the human's personality. The difference is that in the Egyptian book of the dead, the life force and soul take the animal form only after death.

But the Sumerians and Egyptians weren't the only ancient cultures who believed in the afterlife and the land of the dead. A prophet named Zoroaster came to the Middle East long ago, and with him, he brought a religion that came to be known as Zoroastrianism. This new religion spread into India, Russia, and the eastern Balkans; and it was very popular until approximately the seventh century A.D. Today, Zoroastrians are still found in India and Iran.

In the fifth century A.D., the sacred book of Zoroastrianism was written down; it was called the book of Avesta and was written in a mysterious language that nobody has used since that time. The book of Avesta describes Zoroastrianism, teaching that only two gods exist: One is a good god known as Ahura Mazda, and the other is an evil god, known as Angra Mainyu. The good god lives above the skies with his seven angels. The evil god lives beneath the Earth with his demons in the darkness of hell. Ahura Mazda battles Angra Mainyu forever in a battle for the souls of humans.

In Zoroastrianism, when a person dies, his soul remains near his dead body for three days. During this time, the angel (or genie) of justice, Rashnu, judges the soul, along with a god named Mithra. The decision about a man's soul is made at the foot of a bridge leading to the world of the dead. If the soul has been good during the man's life, then the beautiful Daena shows up, and her two guardian dogs lead the soul across the bridge into a house of song. If the soul has been bad, then the soul immediately falls into hell. If the person performed only three more bad acts during life than he performed good acts, his soul is doomed to eternal hell. In an interesting twist from the Sumerians and Egyptians, Zoroastrianism had a third decision branch. What if the man's good deeds exactly equaled his bad deeds during life? In this case, the man's soul went into purgatory, a land called Hammistagan, and nothing—no amount of begging, prayer, or good deeds in Hammistagan—could ever release the soul back to the bridge, where it could be judged again and found suitable for the house of song.

Possibly the most famous land of the dead is called Hades. In fact, Hades was the Greek god of the underworld, which was known as the Kingdom of Hades. When Hades and his brothers, Zeus and Poseidon, defeated their father, Cronus, in battle, they divided the world into three parts. Zeus took the Earth. Poseidon took the seas. And Hades took the land of the dead.

Within Hades, the land of the dead is divided into many regions. One region is called Tartarus, and this is where the evil dead go to be tortured for eternity. Probably because of the evil nature of Tartarus, Hades became known as a synonym for hell. But for the Greeks, Hades was a dreary place where all the dead went, much like the land of the dead in *His Dark Materials*.

In Hades, the souls of the dead are called shades, symbolizing the fact that the ghostly souls are just shadows of their former living selves. The land of the dead called Hades is murky, misty, and dark.

To get to Hades, dead people travel through a series of rivers. Acheron is the river of pain; Cocytus is the river of groaning; Styx, a very famous river which we'll touch upon again in this chapter, is the river of abomination; Lethe is the river of forgetting; and Phlegethon is the river of fire. To get to the rivers, a soul passes through a dark mist called Erebus, though the later Greeks believed that the soul entered through Lake Avernus near Italy.

As with the Sumerians and Egyptians, the Greek soul was ferried across the water by a boatman, in this case called Charon, who dropped the soul at the mouth of the afterworld. The unburied dead didn't make it this far; nor did the dead who lacked sufficient funds to pay Charon. In these sad cases, the souls wandered in misery upon the rivers until the ends of time.

The gate of Hades is guarded (of course), in this case by a three-headed dog named Cerberus. Just as the guardian kept the living from the world of the dead in *His Dark Materials*, Cerberus makes sure the living aren't allowed into Hades. Of course, exceptions always exist to rules, and as Lyra and Will made it past the guardian into the world of the dead, Hercules wrestled Cerberus for entry into Hades, and Orpheus played enchanted music to lull Cerberus into a stupor so Orpheus could pass through the gate. We're also reminded that Lyra offered the harpies wonderful stories to entice them into helping her locate the end border of the world of the dead.

Let's digress briefly and describe the harpies as they existed in the Greek stories of the afterlife. Harpies were thought to be foul birds with the heads and breasts of human women. Just as they are in *His Dark Materials*, harpies had nasty claws and huge wings. They came from the river Styx, mentioned above, and they smelled like rotting death. In a famous Greek legend, harpies tormented the blind King of Thrace by seizing his food before he could eat. The name *harpy* comes from the Greek word meaning "to seize."[95]

So the harpies, who guard the world of the dead in *His Dark Materials*, are derived from the Greek mythology surrounding Hades.

Once in Hades itself, the soul leads an empty existence in a very bleak land. Only the truly wicked are sent to Tartarus for torture; the rest live like the ghosts in *His Dark Materials*, wandering endlessly and listlessly, without purpose.

In later years, the Greeks started to think of Hades as having two realms, an earthly paradise called Elysium, and a hell hole called Dis; and within Dis are realms of horror, with Tartarus at the bottom.

Homer's *Odyssey*, which we all read in high school, is about a near-visit to Hades. In the story, the witch Circe tells Odysseus that he must go to Hades. He's been fighting in the Trojan War for ten years, and to return home, he needs the help of the shade of Tiresias. This particular shade, or shadow/ghost of a dead man, was extremely wise and had lived as both a man and a woman. But to see a shade, of course, requires that Odysseus travel to the world of the dead, or Hades.

At the juncture of the rivers Phlegethon and Cocytus, where they both flow into the river Acheron, Odysseus sacrifices a ram and a ewe at the mouth of a cave. Ghosts flood out of the cave, attracted by the smell of blood, and Odysseus must fight the ghosts until the wise Tiresias appears to drink the blood and speak to Odysseus.

After seeing and speaking to many ghosts of dead people he knew, Odysseus races back down the rivers and far from the

95. Richard Barber and Anne Riches, *Dictionary of Fabulous Beasts*. United Kingdom: Boydell Press, 2000, p. 82.

mouth into hell, or Hades. There's much more to the story, but the idea to be taken here is that Odysseus talks to the ghosts who dwell in the world of the dead—just as Lyra and Will talk to the ghosts who dwell in the world of the dead.

To move more squarely into the Christian theology that underscores *His Dark Materials*, we first must explore some of the concepts of the afterlife proposed by the ancient Jews. A long time ago, these Jews lived between the Jordan River and the Mediterranean, in a region where powerful overlords constantly tried to convert them to other religions. It is thought that between the ninth century B.C. and the second century A.D. the Jews developed the Old Testament, also known as the Five Books of Moses. Eventually, in the second century, the Romans destroyed the bulk of Jewish existence in the region. The ancient Jews had assimilated ideas about the afterlife into their culture for centuries.

Some believed that the world had three levels: Earth, heaven, netherworld. Those who were still alive could seek help and communicate with the dead in the netherworld below and the sky gods in the heavens above. These notions were not incorporated into traditional Judaism.

The second belief in the ancient world of the Jews was that the living do not communicate with the dead. Jews did not seek help from the dead, nor did they worship their dead ancestors. Only the one God was worshipped. No sky gods. The Jews had only one God, who demanded total obedience at all times. This is clearly the more traditional concept of Judaism.

A later belief of the ancient Jews was that the dead souls would indeed live in immortality, and that, someday, all those who suffered terribly in life would be granted freedom from their misery. This belief led to the more traditional Christian view of the afterlife.

As mentioned earlier in this chapter, the ancient Near East

incorporated many cultures; some examples were the Assyrians, Babylonians, Canaanites, Phoenicians, and the early Hebrews. These people were collectively called the Semites by scholars in the eighteenth century. Others in the region, such as the Sumerians, Egyptians, Hittites, and Persians, had cultures that differed greatly from the culture of the Semitic people. And while later Hebrew writers rejected earlier Semitic beliefs about the afterlife, those early beliefs did indeed form a foundation for later Christian views of the afterlife.

The ancient Semitic peoples saw the world in three parts: heaven with the gods; Earth with the people; and the netherworld called Sheol, which housed the dead and the nastier demons. Sheol was dark, misty, and depressing, but it wasn't what we think of as hell. Rather, Sheol was more like the world of the dead in *His Dark Materials*. A god ruled Sheol, and his name was Mot, which literally meant death.

Living humans felt compelled to worship both the gods in heaven and the demons and the dead in Sheol. Temples, sacrifices, prayers, the intervention of prophets and wizards: All were commonplace in the ancient Semitic world. Only the priests knew how to communicate in a truly effective way with the gods in heaven and the dead and gods of the netherworld. Communication with the dead was considered vital for fertility and good crops, among other things. It was so important that the ancient Semites performed rituals in which not only the living got drunk, but it was assumed that the dead got drunk as well.

When a person died, the ancient Semites buried the body in earth or placed it in an underground vault. They felt that this act put the body in contact with the netherworld of Sheol. As the body decayed, a shadowy replica of the dead person emerged and slowly found its way down through the Earth into Sheol, where the shadows of all the dead dwelled. As in *His Dark Materials*, the shadows stayed in Sheol forever; they never faded, they never left for other realms. Those who led moral lives, faithful to ritu-als, survived as shadows in the upper realms of Sheol, where they were closer to Earth and could more easily bestow blessings and offer favors to the living. Those who sinned survived as shadows in the lowest realms of Sheol, where it was harder to help their descendants. In a way, the shadows, who were ghostly images of their living selves, were gods who affected the living.

In return, the living had to offer blessings and perform rituals to help their deceased relatives. If the living failed to offer suffi-cient blessings and offerings, then their deceased relatives sank to the lower realms of Sheol, which were darker and more bleak. It's interesting to note that in the Old Testament, King Saul seeks help from a necromancer to learn the outcome of an up-coming battle. The necromancer, a type of wizard who special-izes in communicating with the dead, digs a hole in the ground to join the world of the living with Sheol. The wizard, a female, then tells King Saul that the shadow ghost of the prophet Samuel has come out of the hole and is ready to talk to the king. She also tells King Saul that only she can see and talk to the prophet directly, so the king has to ask about the battle through her. In the end, she tells King Saul that the prophet knows that the king will die the next day and that all the dead are awaiting the king's shadow in the netherworld. According to the tale, King Saul does indeed die the following day.[96] Here we see that the ghostly dead talk, think, have memories, and have form, just like the living; and just like the ghostly dead in *His Dark Materials*.

Later biblical scholars denounced ancestor worship and necromancy as pagan rituals. As the powerful Assyrians gained more control over and increasingly persecuted the Israelites in the eighth century, religious enthusiasts turned to the notion of one god and only one god. People ceased worshipping the

96. 1 Samuel 28:7.

shadow ghosts of the dead as godlike creatures. They ceased thinking of gods in the heavens and in the netherworlds. King Hezekiah, who reigned between 728 and 699 B.C., instituted various reforms that are noted in the Bible. For example, he demanded that the firstborn sons of the Israelites spend their lives in service to the one god. At this point, the Israelites felt that the one god was in heaven, and only dead humans were in the eternal darkness of Sheol: no demons, no gods, no ghosts.

A century later, in 623 B.C., King Josiah reiterated that the Israelites should worship only one god, and he forbade the worship of all ghosts, dead spirits of any kind, and idols. New laws were enacted to further divide the living from the dead. Previously, people had thought that once a body decomposed and the shadow went to Sheol, the corpse could no longer contaminate living people. Now, people thought that even the dry bones of the dead could contaminate life. Those who still walked upon the Earth avoided all contact with the dead.[97]

After 586 B.C., when their kingdom was destroyed, the Israelites started wondering if God would indeed save them from the eternal darkness of Sheol. Surely, there must be more than suffering in life and then suffering forever in death. The author of Psalm 73 suggests that the riches of the sinners don't buy them anything in Sheol, but on the other hand, their sinning doesn't buy them any pain either. He wonders what the good man has that the wicked lacks. He suggests that after death, all we'll have is God in heaven. In Psalm 49, another author claims that the sinners will not be able to bargain with God, that they will be sent into the lowest depths of Sheol to suffer for eternity. On the other hand, says the author of Psalm 49, the pious and the faithful will survive the darkness of Sheol. Together, the psalmists expressed the hope that God would receive the righteous after

97. Job 14:21; also Isaiah 63:16, and others.

death. The concept of heaven in the afterlife was renewed. The wicked went to Sheol; the good went to heaven.

In addition, the Greek influence of the immortal soul resurfaced. Rather than survive as a shadow ghost of one's former self, the Greeks suggested another idea, that the dead person's immortal soul survived intact, and that the soul would either remain in bliss forever or suffer endlessly in torment.

Ancient writers such as Plato (428–347 B.C.) and Cicero (106–43 B.C.) suggested that the Isles of the Blest were located in heaven, which existed beyond the stars. Plato believed that the soul was the person's life force, and after death, the soul was finally released from imprisonment in the body, only to become stronger and more whole. The soul then rose into the sky and from there reached into the heavens to find its final home. This is somewhat similar to the notion of the ghosts in *His Dark Materials*, who are finally freed from the world of the dead, dissolve into the sky, and float into the heavens to find their final homes. It is also somewhat similar to the notion of souls in *His Dark Materials*, which fracture and float to the heavens, rejoining the rest of the cosmic dark material. According to the ancient writer Philo, the righteous soul becomes immortal and incorporeal, and it joins the angels in heaven. In *His Dark Materials*, the souls and ghosts are all part of the cosmic consciousness, the oneness known as the dark matter. (For further explanation, please see Chapter 2, "Dust, Dark Matter, Dark Energy, and Other Celestial Things.")

So by the first century A.D., the Jews held several different views about the afterlife. The early Christians chimed in with yet another idea. These newer images of the afterlife were constructed by Jesus, Paul, and the author of the Book of Revelation, among others. Basically, they held that the key to the afterlife was making sure you led a Christian life so you could end up in heaven, enjoying eternal bliss with complete knowledge of God.

The darkness of Sheol was replaced by hopes for the pure light of heaven and God. Early Christians were less concerned with life on Earth than they were with eternal joy with God in heaven.

Saul of Tarsus converted to become the Christian missionary Paul. He wrote in the New Testament that those who will not get into the kingdom of God include "unrepentant fornicators, idolators, adulterers, homosexuals, thieves, drunkards, slanderers, swindlers, sorcerers, the envious, the quarrelsome, the indecent, and the greedy."[98] Mark later talks of eternal damnation for those who renounce the Holy Ghost.

John writes of the conflict between God and the powers of evil, known as Satan. At the time John wrote, Satan was equivalent to the Roman Empire. The Book of Revelation begins with a vision of heaven and ends with a vision in which heaven and Earth coincide. Rather than focus on eternal damnation, John writes of the splendors and beauty of heaven. Gestured into heaven by an angel, John saw God in human form sitting upon a divine throne. The splendor of God on his throne was more dazzling than all the jewels in the world, shone more brightly and with more colors than the rainbow. Spirits were guarding the throne, and on either side of God's throne were twelve smaller thrones, one for each elder who was wearing a white gown and a golden crown. A host of angels filled the background. The winged spirits sang constantly: "Holy, holy, holy is the Lord God Almighty; he was, he is, and he is to come." Heaven is viewed as a human place: There are twenty-four elders there, corresponding to the twenty-four families of Jewish priests. As angels flock to the scene, the Christ appears as a "lamb that seemed to be sacrificed." Eventually 144,000 people join the scene, from all the

---

98. Alice K. Turner, *The History of Hell*. New York: Harcourt Brace & Company, 1993, p. 52. If you're interested in the development of philosophies related to hell throughout the ages, this book is an excellent resource.

tribes of Israel, as well as a near-infinite number of people from all religions, races, tribes, and nations. One of the heavenly elders tells the visionary that the people are all martyrs who died for the Christian faith.

John also describes the activities of the angels; for example, Michael and his angels fight Satan and his demons; other angels blow trumpets, and so forth. After the forces of light defeat the forces of darkness, God will establish an eternal kingdom and all souls will live forever in peace.

For this book, it suffices to point out that, while John suggests that the angels will destroy the evil forces of Satan, the angels unite with Will and Lyra (Adam and Eve) to destroy the evil forces of the Authority (not God, but rather, the first angel, who then created all other angels; an Authority who was presumed in *His Dark Materials* to be the godlike creator).

There is no heaven, per se, in *His Dark Materials*. There is only the cosmic consciousness, the forever, and all the dark matter. And there also is no hell in *His Dark Materials*; for hell exists in the form of life on the billions of parallel worlds.

There is a form of purgatory, the Sheol, the limbo nothingness where all ghost shadows go after the body dies. The world of the dead in *His Dark Materials* is much like purgatory, with one crucial difference: In purgatory, the soul (not the ghost) still has a chance to escape to heaven or to sink into hell. In *His Dark Materials*, the ghost shadow remains in purgatory forever. There is no escape until Will and Lyra lead the ghosts from the underworld through a cave and back onto Earth, where the ghosts then dissolve in glee and float off to rejoin all the dark matter in the cosmos.

8

SPEC+ERS, VAMPIRES, NIGH+ GHAS+S, AND ZOMBIES

In the last chapter, we discussed the ghost shadows in the world of the dead. But there are some other ghostlike creatures in *His Dark Materials* as well. These are known as specters.

Every time a window opens to another world, a specter is created (*The Amber Spyglass*, page 486). Nobody really knows where the specters come from or what they are made of. All that is known is that, as the bonds of the smallest particles of matter break (for example, by opening a window into another world), something comes undone, and that something enables the specters to slip into other worlds.

The specters are abundant in the world of Cittàgazze, where adult souls are basically consumed by specters. The specters "eat the life out of" the adults (*The Amber Spyglass*, page 60). After the specters eat them, the adults are empty: as if they are now zombies with vacant eyes and no reaction to pinching and poking.

In fact, according to Ma Costa, there are several kinds of ghosts, or specters, in Lyra's world. The Windsuckers draw all the strength out of a person, and the Breathless Ones are half-dead warriors who can't die but who aren't alive, either (*The Golden Compass*, page 107).

Some people, including Serafina the witch, think of specters as vampires, which also drink the life from people. Vampires drink a person's blood, while specters drink a person's life force, or soul (*The Amber Spyglass*, page 130).

The traditional definition of a ghost, or specter, is that it is the spirit of a dead person. In ancient times, the word *ghost* referred to disembodied souls. It was thought that when a person died, his soul went to the underworld (see Chapter 7, "The Afterlife: Hell, Harpies, and Heaven"), and there, various things happened to the souls based on the particular culture. Melanesians, for example, thought that the soul then divided into the *aunga*, or good part, and the *adaro*, or the ghostly bad part. The *adaro* returned to the live body's home on a ship of the dead, or sometimes the *adaro* simply scooted across the ground until reaching its destination.

Some Chinese people believe that the soul has three parts: a good part, a bad part, and a third part that stays in the ancestral altar forever, so the family can bless it. In many cultures, it is assumed that the souls of deceased family members dwell in the house with the living.

Ghosts are sometimes visible, though usually they're considered to be apparitions: vague, shadowy creatures, much as they are in *His Dark Materials*. Ghosts make strange noises, they cause objects to move and doors to slam, they create drafts.

Some ghosts return to avenge their deaths; others return to provide critical information to the living; still others return to reenact their deaths. Some come back to protect their children and spouses, some to punish enemies, some to complete unfinished business.

In western cultures, the soul supposedly goes to heaven or hell, so the return of the soul in the form of a ghost is a frightening thing. In fact, the ghost may be a demonic, evil spirit if it returns from hell to haunt somebody's house. Some people think of ghosts as souls from purgatory, who return to ask the living for help. Others think of ghosts as demons who are pretending to be dead people.

In Eastern Europe, some people think the returning dead are vampires. This is what Serafina suggests in *His Dark Materials*.

Vampire lore has been around since ancient times. People in cultures all over the world have believed in these blood-sucking creatures. The ancient Chaldeans in Mesopotamia believed in vampires, as did the ancient Assyrians, who wrote about vampires on clay and stone tablets.

In China, vampires are often portrayed as red-eyed monsters with green hair. In ancient India, vampire legends were evident from the paintings on cave walls of blood-drinking creatures. In some writings in 1500 B.C., the destroyer Rakshasas is depicted as a vampire; and paintings from 3000 B.C. show the Lord of Death drinking blood from a human skull. The Indian Baital vampire is a mythological monster who hangs upside down from trees, much like a bat. The Baital hasn't any blood of its own.

The ancient Malaysians had a vampire called the Penannggalen, which was a human head with entrails. The entrails left the Penannggalen's head to seek the blood of human infants. In ancient Peru, the *canchus* were devil worshippers who drank blood from children.

In ancient Babylonia, the *ekimmu* was a vampire spirit who drank human blood when hungry. In Wallachia, the *murony* vampire sucked blood and operated as a shapeshifter, changing from human to dog to insect to cat at will. Sometimes the *murony* operated in werewolf form.

In Greece, vampires were thought to be winged serpents combined with human females. The ancient Greek *strigoe* or *lamiae* were monsters who drank the blood of children. These notions came largely from the lore of Lamia, one of Zeus's lovers; when Hera fought Lamia, the mistress went insane and killed all her own children; then at night she killed everyone else's children as well.

From the far east, vampire lore spread from China, Tibet, India, and the Mediterranean to the coast of the Black Sea, and from there to Greece and the Carpathian mountains, Hungary, and Transylvania.

Most vampires in film and literature are based on the Eastern European variety, that of a blood-sucking, sexy creature who returns from the dead. These vampires wear gorgeous clothes and sumptuous capes, and they can turn into bats at will.

Some of the richest vampire lore comes from Russia, Bulgaria, Serbia, and Poland: the Slavic peoples. The word *vampir* is related to the Russian word *peets*: to drink. When the Slavs migrated from north of the Black Sea, they started converting to Christianity. During the ninth and tenth centuries, the Eastern Orthodox Church and the Western Roman Catholic Church were battling for overall control of Christianity. In 1054, the two churches formally divided from each other, and the Russians, Serbians, and Bulgarians went with the Eastern Orthodox Church, while the Croatians, Poles, and Czechs went with the Roman Catholic Church. The Eastern Orthodox faction decided that the living dead were vampires.

In the beginning, the Slavic people thought that vampires were created from people who were born "on the wrong day," who died under strange circumstances, who were excommunicated from the church, who were buried improperly. Some also believed that people born with tails or odd teeth could end up being vampires.

To protect the dead from turning into vampires, the deceased were buried with crucifixes, with their chins held upright with blocks, and with poppy seeds so the numerically obsessed vampires could count and count rather than cause trouble. Other dead were pierced with stakes to protect them. Yet others had their clothes nailed to the sides of their coffins.

To destroy vampires who were roaming the countryside, sucking the blood from villagers, people used stakes, holy water, and exorcism. They also decapitated presumed vampires and burned them. Garlic left in the church was said to expose vampires. Later methods of destroying a vampire included driving a stake through its heart, decapitating the remains, and putting garlic into the mouth. Later methods became more gruesome, including bullets, dismemberment of the body, and burning the remains, with the ashes given to people as preventive medicine.

In Romania, vampires were known as *strigoli*, from the Roman word *strix*, which referred to the screech owl. It was thought that the *strix* were demons. Of the various forms of *strigoli*, the *strigoli vii* were live witches who became vampires after they died; and the *strigoli mort* were reanimated dead. There was also a *vircolac*, a type of wolf who ate the sun and moon; this type of demonic being later became known as a werewolf.

Speaking of owls, Lilith supposedly was a monster who roamed at night as an owl. Adam's wife before Eve, Lilith supposedly became a demon because she demanded that Adam respect her opinions. In fact, the myth has it that she killed babies and pregnant women at night using her owl form. Later it was thought that Lilith became a vampire who attacked all of Adam and Eve's children.

In the English language, the word *vampyre* or *vampire* was first noted in the early 1700s. It may have come from the Turkish *uber*, meaning witch, and from there to the Slavic *upior* or *upyr*, which became vampyre.

The Eastern European nosferatu also referred to the vampire. The western world learned of nosferatu when Bram Stoker wrote his famous novel *Dracula*.

In the middle ages, many people blamed the black death—the bubonic plague—on vampires. The plague killed perhaps one-third of Europe's population and was actually spread by fleas and rats.

In the eighteenth century, a major vampire scare broke out across Eastern Europe. Peter Plogojowitz died when he was 62 years old, but he supposedly returned a few times after dying to beg his son for food. His son refused to help the dead Plogojowitz and was soon found dead himself, followed by several neighbors, all of whom died from massive blood loss. Another famous case of vampirism from this period involved Arnold Paole, a farmer who had been attacked by a vampire while collecting hay and died. Soon after Paole's death, the local farmers and villagers began to die as well. Government officials examined the bodies of both Plogojowitz and Paole, and their reports were distributed throughout Europe. Terrified of vampires, people began digging up bodies to examine them for evidence of the undead blood-sucking killers. In 1746, Austrian Empress Maria Theresa asked her personal doctor to conduct an investigation into vampirism. He concluded that vampires did *not* exist, and the scare died down.

We need not dwell on the subject of vampires in this book. Our only point, after all, is that Serafina notes that the specters are very similar to vampires, and we concur that specters and vampires both suck the life force out of the living.

As for the indication that the specters in *His Dark Materials* turn people into zombies, this also seems to be drawn from the folklore of our real world. Zombies in *His Dark Materials* are people from whom specters have sucked life; they are soulless people, those without human consciousness.

In our world, the notion of zombies originated with Haitian Voodoo culture. The word *zombie* comes from the Haitian word *zombi*, which means spirit of the dead. As the story goes, Voodoo priests called *bokors* studied enough black magic to figure out how to resurrect the dead using a powder called *coup padre*.

The primary ingredient of *coup padre* is deadly tetrodotoxin from the porcupine fish, the fou-fou. The tetrodotoxin disrupts communication in the brain and is 500 times more deadly than cyanide. A tiny drop of tetrodotoxin can kill a man.

This weird poison, *coup padre*, was made by first burying a bouga toad (called a *bufo marinus*) and a sea snake in a jar. After the toad and snake died from the rage of being confined in the jar, the bokor extracted their venom. The toad's glands held bufogenin and bufotoxin, each being from 50 to 100 times more deadly than digitalis. The bufogenin and bufotoxin increased the victim's heartbeat. In addition, the glands held bufotenine, a powerful hallucinogenic drug.

To these drugs, the bokor added millipedes and tarantulas to tcha-tcha seeds that caused pulmonary edema, nontoxic consigne seeds, pomme cajou (cashew) leaves, and bresillet tree leaves. Both of these types of leaves were related to poison ivy. Having ground everything into a powder, the bokor buried the concoction for two days, after which he added ground tremblador and desmember plants; two plants from the stinging nettle family, which injected formic acid-like chemicals beneath the victim's skin; and dieffenbachia with its glasslike needles, which made the victim's throat swell, causing great difficulty in breathing and talking. He then added the sharp needles of the bwa pine.

But we're not done yet. . . .

The bokor next added poisonous animals to the deadly powder. Two species of tarantulas were ground up and added to the skins of white tree frogs. Another bouga toad went into the mixture, followed by four types of puffer fish, the fou-fou carrying the *coup padre*. The final ingredient was dead human flesh.

If a family or community despised someone sufficiently, they called upon the bokor to turn that person into a zombie.

After ingesting the *coup padre*, the despised villager or family member immediately became numb. His lips and tongue went numb first, followed by his fingers, arms, toes, and legs; then his entire body went numb. He was sick with feelings of weakness, floating, nausea, vomiting, diarrhea, stomach pain, and headaches. The victim's pulse picked up, he had trouble walking and talking; and finally, paralysis set in: His breathing became shallow, his heart nearly ceased to beat, and his body temperature plummeted. The victim's body was blue, his eyes were glassy. In essence, the victim was in a coma.

While still alive, the poor, despised victim was buried as if already dead. Because he wasn't really dead, the victim often heard his own funeral and had to suffer through his own burial.

Later the bokor dug up the body and brought the person back to life. Physically, the person appeared as he had before ingesting the *coup padre*, but his mind was gone and his soul was dead. Traumatized, the victim believed he had been reanimated, brought back to life. As a mindless drone, this new zombie remained under the bokor's power and did the bokor's bidding. The bokor gave his new zombie a hallucinogenic mixture of datura stramonium, cane sugar, and sweet potato. There is no antidote for tetrodotoxin, so once a zombie, always a zombie.

In the Haitian culture, the zombie has no human consciousness and free will. He's much like the zombie created by the specters in *His Dark Materials*. What the *coup padre* does, the specter does.

The final bit of weirdness associated with demonic creatures from our own cultures comes in the form of the night ghasts and cliff ghasts. Lyra first mentions the night ghasts on page 50 of *The Golden Compass*. A night ghast awakens her, and she sees three headless creatures in her bedroom. Much later in the book,

Lyra and Lee Scoresby encounter the cliff ghasts (*The Golden Compass*, page 320), who have frog mouths, bulging eyes, leathery wings, and hooked claws.

The ghasts are much the same as the harpies (see Chapter 7), except that they have frog mouths rather than human female heads, and they don't have breasts. The word *ghast* means "to scare" someone or something.

In the world of H. P. Lovecraft, the ghasts are a race of creatures from the Dreamlands. According to Sandy Peterson's *Field Guide to Cthulhu Monsters*, a ghast "is a great floundering whitish thing with a black-furred back and distinct traces of human ancestry in its noseless, bulging-lipped face."[99] It has long, wide legs, hooked claws, but no leathery wings.

You can think of the ghasts as breastless harpies with frog faces. Or you can think of them as garden-variety ghouls, set in the worlds of *His Dark Materials* to give us the creeps.

99. Sandy Peterson, *Field Guide to Cthulhu Monsters: A Field Observer's Handbook of Preternatural Entities*. Hayward, California: Chaosium, Inc., 1988, p. 32.

PART 2

BACK MATTER

AUR⊕RA B⊕REALIS (N⊕R+HERN LIGH+S)

9

In *His Dark Materials*, Lord Asriel uses scientific instruments to harness the power of the Aurora Borealis, or Northern Lights, and to cut the bonds between humans and their daemons. When Lord Asriel uses his machines to try to sever soul from person, enormous energy is released that opens a window through the Aurora Borealis into a parallel world.

According to Lord Asriel, the glowing particles of the Aurora Borealis aren't really caused by light; rather, they're caused by Dust (see Chapter 2, "Dust, Dark Matter, Dark Energy, and Other Celestial Things"). In the Dust shown in a photogram of the Northern Lights is a child (*The Golden Compass*, page 21). We learn later that behind the curtain of the Northern Lights is a parallel world: a city in the sky.

The description of the Northern Lights in *The Golden Compass* is that of "streams and veils of light" that hang "like curtains, looped and festooned on invisible hooks hundreds of miles high or blowing out sideways in the stream of some unimaginable wind" (*The Golden Compass*, page 22). Lord Asriel explains that the Northern Lights are composed of solar rays and storms of charged particles in all colors of the rainbow. Later, Lyra and her daemon, Pan, see the Aurora in the northern sky: transparent, shimmering, gently swaying curtains of light in all colors (*The Golden Compass*, page 184). And she hears the Aurora Borealis, as well: it crackles and rustles (*The Golden Compass*, page 382).

In this chapter, we discuss the real Aurora Borealis, or Northern Lights. What are they, and what creates them? What makes up the colors and the lights?

Aurora Borealis, meaning "dawn of the North" in Latin, is the scientific name for the Northern Lights. In the southern hemisphere, the lights are known as the Aurora Australis, or "dawn of the South."

Studies of the auroras began in the nineteenth century, when explorers reached into the vast regions of the Arctic and Antarctic, where few people lived. Norwegian explorer Fridtjof Nansen (1861–1930) studied the Aurora Borealis and tried to explain it with words and pictures. He wrote that the Northern Lights appeared as a supernatural image, "flashing in matchless power and beauty over the sky in all the colours of the rainbow. . . . The prevailing one at first was yellow, but that gradually flickered over to green, and then a sparkling ruby-red began to show at the bottom of the rays on the under side of the arch. And now from the faraway western horizon a fiery serpent writhed itself up over the sky, shining brighter and brighter as it came. It split into three, all brilliantly glittering. Then the colours changed. . . . Sheaves of rays swept along the side of the serpents, driven through the ether-like waves before a storm wind. . . ."[100]

Later, British explorer Robert F. Scott (1868–1912) was try-

100. Fridtjof Nansen, *Furthest North*. London: Constable, 1904, p. 160. Quoted in Harald Falck-Ytter, *Aurora: The Northern Lights in Mythology, History, and Science*, originally published in Germany, 1983; paperback English edition, New York: Bell Pond Books, 1999, p. 11.

ing to reach the South Pole when he discovered the Aurora Australis and wrote, "The eastern sky was swaying with auroral light, the most vivid and beautiful display that I had ever seen—fold on fold the arches and curtains of vibrating luminosity rose and spread across the sky, to slowly fade and yet again spring to glowing life. . . . It is impossible to witness such a beautiful phenomenon without a sense of awe, and yet this sentiment is not inspired by its brilliancy but rather by its delicacy in light and colour, its transparency, and above all by its tremulous evanescence of form."[101]

It is this beauty, this shifting wondrous display of light and color, that Lord Asriel sees, that Lyra sees, that provides the backbone of *His Dark Materials*. Trying to determine the causes of the Northern Lights, Lord Asriel discovers that, like everything else in *His Dark Materials*, they consist of Dust, that dark matter of the universe that opens possibilities . . . and doors to other universes. In reality, we know much about the Northern Lights—how they're formed, what they're made of—though the possibility remains that dark matter may play a role.

Just as Lord Asriel supplies photograms of the Northern Lights, our scientists have taken photographs over the years. German physicist Martin Brendal took the first photograph in 1892.

Just like the scientists in Lord Asriel's world, at the beginning of the nineteenth century our scientists were trying to determine the causes of the aurora's magnetic and electrical power. Mathematics and astronomy professor Christopher Hansteen, who worked at the University of Christiania-Oslo, went to Siberia to study the strong geomagnetic fields. He noticed that the horizontal aspects of the magnetic fields increased directly before the aurora flamed. He also noticed that the horizontal aspects de-

101. Robert F. Scott, *Scott's Last Expedition*. London: Murray, 1927, p. 257. Quoted in Harald Falck-Ytter, op. cit.

creased when the aurora died down. He proved that the Northern Lights were directly related to the Earth's magnetism.

Then in 1827, French physicist Jean B. Biot studied the aurora on the Shetland Islands in Scotland. Biot used a polarimeter but found no traces of polarization. He concluded that the Northern Lights were far more than a simple reflection of the sun.

During the time of Biot, scientists were also studying the Aurora Borealis using spectral analysis. A spectrum originates when light shines through a prism and divides into colored bands. Instruments calibrate the spectrum into wavelengths of different colors, which are related to substances, such as gases, in the object being measured. Swedish physicist Anders Jonas Ångström used a spectrometer to study the aurora and concluded that it consisted of luminous gases. The lights and colors were not caused by water and ice: they were caused by these luminous gases. (If Ångström's name sounds familiar to you, it's because he measured the yellow-green dominant color line in the spectrogram of the Northern Lights, and based on how he measured this color, his measurement became famous as one ten millionth of a millimeter, or one angstrom. He gave the yellow-green line 5,567 units of length: 5,567 angstroms.)

In 1859, Richard C. Carrington, a theologian with a private observatory, determined that solar flares connected to sunspots were directly related to the Northern Lights. He was peering at sunspots in his telescope when a huge magnetic storm hit the entire Earth, creating an aurora that could be seen all over the world.

In 1882 and 1883, Danish physicist Sophus Tromholt was in charge of two Norwegian observatories in Lapland. He described auroral ovals, which we'll talk about later in this chapter; yet his work did not contribute significantly to the study of the auroras during his lifetime. It's worth noting that, as early as 1879, Tromholt determined that the auroral oval spreads toward the equator every eleven years, corresponding to the increase in sunspots every eleven years.

In reality, the Aurora Borealis originates with our sun. Explosions and flares inside the sun throw huge amounts of solar particles into outer space as plasma clouds (in plasma, the temperature is so high that molecules disintegrate into charged particles). The plasma clouds race at 200 to 1,500 kilometers per second (as with all estimates, the numbers vary slightly depending on researcher), and about two or three days later they reach Earth. As they approach the planet, the Earth's magnetosphere, which serves as a protecting shield and field of energy processes above the Earth, captures the plasma clouds and sends them to the north and south poles. As researcher Robert H. Eather wrote: "Modern understanding of the aurora is tied up with our understanding of the magnetosphere as a whole. . . . [The magnetosphere] describes the region of near Earth space that is threaded by magnetic field lines linked to the Earth and in which very hot or ionized gas dominates over the neutral atmosphere. . . . It is populated with ions and electrons originating in both the Earth's atmosphere and the sun's atmosphere."[102]

The identification of the magnetosphere led to the discovery of solar plasma, also called the solar wind, in 1959. The solar plasma is a stream of electrically neutral particles shooting at the speed of light but behaving like a plasma substance. What this means is scientists can measure and count the particles, even though the particles are extremely tiny and densely collected. The solar wind races at 200 to 1,500 kilometers per second (up to 950 miles per second), and compared to light at 300,000 kilometers or 186,000 miles per second, the solar wind moves at a relatively slow pace.

102. R. H. Eather, *Majestic Lights*. Washington, D.C.: American Geophysical Union, 1980, p. 217.

Of interest in relation to *His Dark Materials*, the solar plasma fills the solar system, and beyond Saturn it forms a shield from the deadly cosmic radiation of the outer realms. We note that dark matter aka Dust as well as dark energy also fills the solar system; so it's conceivable that the Dust in *His Dark Materials* indeed does contribute to the Northern Lights. In the case of solar plasma, it consists of ionized hydrogen and helium. As discussed in Chapter 2 of this book, some people theorize that the dark matter consists of hydrogen gas clouds; but most scientists dismiss hydrogen as dark matter for the simple reason that we can observe hydrogen gas using radio, optical, ultraviolet, infrared, and X-ray telescopes. With solar plasma, the electrons and protons of the ionized hydrogen and helium transport the sun's magnetic energy and lines of magnetic force throughout space.

As the plasma clouds move toward the two poles, Earth's atmosphere shields us from the solar particles. As the particles stop in the atmosphere, they collide with atmospheric gases and emit photons. Because the atmosphere is being bombarded by a cloud of these solar particles, there are millions and millions of these collisions, and rather than see a little light, we see curtains of light from the Earth. This is the Aurora Borealis: curtains and veils of lights that stream across the sky. It takes a minimum of 100 million photons to create an Aurora Borealis that we can see with the naked eye.

In the middle of the sun, the temperature is more than 15 million degrees Kelvin. The pressure inside the sun is 250 billion times greater than the pressure on the surface of the Earth, and the sun's surface is 5,800 degrees Kelvin. Inside the sun, heat turns hydrogen into helium.

Every eleven years or so, the number of sunspots peaks, and during this period, more solar particles are thrown into deep space than when the sunspots are at a lull. When the sun has more spots, the Earth has more auroras. In 2001–2002, the sunspots peaked, and hence, we saw magnificent displays of the Northern Lights here on Earth. Now we have to wait until 2011–2012 for the next peak!

At supersonic speeds, the sun constantly emits electron-and-ion gases in what is known as the solar wind. This is a strong wind, whipping fiercely, and when it reaches Earth, the Aurora display is vivid and much closer to the equator than usual.

In 1881, the Swiss physicist Herman Fritz wrote *Das Polarlicht*, a book about the Northern Lights. In his book, Fritz claimed that at 67 degrees north, the Northern Lights are most intense, and he pegged this as the auroral zone. During the 1960s, satellites mapped the auroral zones in more detail. We found that the auroras appear as oval circles with magnetic poles in the centers. These oval circles, for both northern and southern lights actually, are known as the auroral zones. It is here that the auroras are most intense, vivid, and colorful.

At midnight, the auroral oval is twice as far from the magnetic pole and twice as wide as it is at noon. As the sunspots intensify, the aurora oval enlarges and spreads toward the equator. In addition, brilliant auroras can be observed approximately once every twenty-seven days; this is because the active sunspot areas of the sun face the Earth approximately every twenty-seven days. Also, it's more likely that you'll see the Northern Lights right before winter sets in and right after winter starts thawing into spring. If you're in the Mediterranean, you may see the Northern Lights only once every century. If you live on the equator, you'll see them once every two hundred years; that is, if modern medicine enables you to live that long! The best places for seeing the Aurora Borealis are in Norway and Alaska. If you're in northern Norway, you'll see brilliant displays of the Northern Lights in February, March, and October. In Andenes, Norway, you can see the lights any night that's dark and clear; in Fairbanks, Alaska, you can see them approximately ten times a month; and in Oslo,

Norway, maybe three nights every month. If you live near the U.S.-Canadian border, look for the Northern Lights two to four times a year.

In 1896, Norwegian researcher Kristian Birkeland suggested that electrically charged particles from the sun reach the Earth's magnetic field almost at light speed, where they then traverse magnetic lines of force to both poles. The electrically charged particles zip along spiral paths, reach the Earth's atmosphere, and turn luminous. Birkeland even calculated the paths of the electron particles and other details; and his work became the basis of future geophysics and aurora research.[103]

After taking 40,000 parallactic auroral pictures between 1910 and 1940, mathematician Carl Størmer determined that the average height of the aurora was between 100 and 120 kilometers. At night, most auroras were between 90 and 150 kilometers.[104] Like Lord Asriel's technique, Størmer's photography used a very fast lens and a special plate sensitive to violet. He was able to take photos with an exposure time below one second.

Since Størmer's time, scientists have used sensitive light meters known as auroral photometers to measure the height of the auroras. They've found that the upper edge of the lights stretches higher than was shown by Størmer's measurements. In fact, red auroral rays may reach beyond 500 kilometers.

As for the colors of the Northern Lights, they appear as bands and spectral lines in the visible, ultraviolet, and infrared

103. For a detailed account of Birkeland's work, see Lucy Jago, *The Northern Lights: The True Story of the Man Who Unlocked the Secrets of the Aurora Borealis*. New York: Alfred A. Knopf, Inc., 2001.
104. Harald Falck-Ytter, op. cit., page 77. Slightly different numbers are supplied at: http://www.northern-lights.no/. And other, very similar numbers are given by Candace Savage, *Aurora: The Mysterious Northern Lights*. Buffalo, NY: Firefly Books, 2001, p. 100. The numbers supplied in the main text are very close approximates and certainly suffice for our purposes.

ranges. In contrast, the sun radiates in all visible colors, which is why sunlight appears white.

When electrically charged particles excite atmospheric gases, electrons shift orbit inside the atoms: The charged particles release energy because they are unstable, and the energy they release is emitted as light. The illumination at different altitudes is caused by the various velocities of the charged particles as they penetrate the atmosphere.

Some researchers claim that, at 120 to 180 kilometers, the aurora is full of green. Other researchers say that the green oxygen line is strongest between 100 and 240 kilometers. Above 240 kilometers, red is seen (though again, some researchers claim that the red is prevalent at 180 kilometers and above rather than 240 kilometers and above). Blue and violet are seen below 100 to 120 kilometers. If the sun has a lot of activity, the entire aurora may appear red. While the numbers may vary from researcher to researcher, the appearance of the different colors at different altitudes is always given the same way: red in the highest reaches of the aurora, green beneath, and the blues and violets below; and during very intense solar activity, far more red throughout the display.

On clear winter nights, a weak aurora may appear as a diffuse band of light. If the aurora is of medium strength, it is brighter than most stars and blocks the view of stars beyond it. Strong Northern Lights are as strong as the light from the moon.

The auroras appear in a variety of forms, such as a homogeneous band, which spans the sky in east-to-west arcs; the homogeneous arc, which is one east-to-west arc about 1,000 kilometers long and 10 kilometers wide; an arc with ray structures, which looks like the homogeneous arc with the addition of rays shooting off the arc; the band with structure, which consists of one or more distinct thick bands stretching from the east to the west; a series of rays shooting up along the Earth's magnetic field, with the rays varying in rapid patterns, which are seen when the sun is very active; coronas, also seen when the sun is very active, which shoot rays up in rapidly changing fan formations; and curtains, as in *His Dark Materials*, in which the widths of the auroral bands and the lengths of the rays fill the entire sky, while waves of rapidly changing colors and light undulate. There are other structures as well: Spirals, pulsations, and diffuse surfaces may fill the sky.

As for the sounds Lyra hears from the Northern Lights, these sounds are considered real by some researchers, impossible by others. Over the centuries, people have reported auroral sounds such as whizzing, crackling, and hissing noises. Because the lights are not associated with vibrations and movements that we ordinarily hear, scientists cannot explain how the auroras make sounds. If sound waves are present, it would take them five minutes to travel from the Northern Lights to the ground, yet the reports of sounds have them occurring at the same time the visions of the auroras are viewed.

Scientists provide various theories about auroral sounds, of course, but none have been proven, and no sounds have been recorded. The issue remains a mystery.

As we move into the future, we'll learn far more about the Northern Lights. Tomorrow's research will require advanced instruments operating on satellites and rockets. Who knows what we'll learn? Will we find that the solar plasma is related to dark matter and dark energy? Will we find that the power of the Northern Lights can be used to harness the power of the dark matter and energy? Today, there's no way to know, but the future can bring almost anything.

WEIRD SCIENCE, PART I

10

In this chapter and the one that follows we tie up some of the loose threads surrounding *His Dark Materials*. We refer to these sections as weird science, but they could just as easily be called weird fantasy or weird mythology. Because most of the subjects are presented as science and technology in *His Dark Materials*, we lump them together as topics of weird science.

A prime example is Lyra's alethiometer, a scientific device that is intimately connected to dark matter, dark energy, and cosmic consciousness. Another example is the Gallivespian's Lodestone Resonator, which is a telecommunications device that appears to operate on some form of quantum entanglement—don't worry, I'll tell you what that is in the section about the Lodestone Resonator!

Other pseudo-scientific topics include mechanical insects and dragonfly spies, zeppelins, and gyrocopters. And in the next chapter, we take a look at some final matters, such as the I Ching and shamanism. You can see why I called these final two chapters "Weird Science."

First, let's take a look at the alethiometer, a device that's driven by Dust. Answering questions that are inside Lyra's mind, it operates using symbols, and each of its many symbols has a wide variety of meanings.

Although it's rather heavy, the alethiometer is tiny and fits in Lyra's hand. It looks like a clock or compass; hence, the title of the first book, *The Golden Compass*. Its hands point to various locations around a dial, and in those locations are tiny pictures. At first glance, Lyra sees an anchor, an hourglass with a skull, a beehive, and several other pictures; in all, she sees thirty-six symbols on the dial.

Lyra figures that her alethiometer is made from brass and crystal, though it shines as if made from gold. When he gives the alethiometer to Lyra, the Master explains that only six alethiometers have ever been created, that it tells the truth, and that it's very hard to learn how to read it (*The Golden Compass*, page 78).

The alethiometer is an instrument we all wish we had. It helps Lyra foresee what's going to happen in the future, and it helps her understand the past.

As she plays with it, she realizes that it has three tiny wheels, each of which turns one of three hands. The hands click into place as they move around the dial. A fourth hand moves on its own like the needle of a compass, out of Lyra's control (*The Golden Compass*, pages 78–79).

Lyra studies the alethiometer, playing with it whenever she has spare time. According to Farder Coram, each picture is a symbol that stands for all sorts of things. For example, he explains, the anchor's first meaning is that a person must maintain her hope; the second meaning of the anchor is that the person must not waver with decisions; the third meaning has to do with preventing something; the fourth has to do with the sea; and according to Farder Coram, each symbol may be composed of an endless number of meanings: It all depends on how the user manipulates the hands and interprets the alethiometer's clues (*The Golden Compass*, page 126).

The alethiometer operates much like an oracle or ouija board, which is used by kids for fun and by adults to seek the truth using spiritualism. All the letters of the alphabet are inscribed on the ouija board, which also has words such as Yes, No, and Maybe on it. The person attempting to read and interpret communications from the ouija board places her fingers on a three-legged device called a planchette. If others are present, they may also place their fingers on the planchette. Nobody moves the planchette; they wait for the board to move it. The truthseeker asks the board a question. If all is working well, the ouija board responds by moving the planchette to letters that spell an answer; or the board responds by moving the planchette over Yes, No, or Maybe.

The Greek word for truth happens to be *aletheia*, and the suffix of meter implies measurement (*metron* in Greek means measure). Alethiology is the branch of philosophy that deals with truth. In fact, an alethoscope is an instrument for viewing pictures. Literally, an alethiometer is a truth measurement.

Like the ouija board and other oracles, the alethiometer speaks in riddles. The ancient Greeks actually did believe in the power of oracles and had a famous oracle monitored by priests and priestesses at Delphi. If you wanted to learn if your boyfriend loved you, if you were going to inherit wealth, if your beloved at war was going to die, if your disease would be cured, or whatever, you could visit the oracle at Delphi. There, you would make offerings to the gods and ask the priests and priestesses for help. They would consult the oracle and get back to you.

The priests and priestesses of the oracle at Delphi were like today's fortune tellers and tarot card readers. It was well known that Nancy Reagan, wife of President Ronald Reagan, had a private fortune teller who gave her advice. The daily newspapers are full of horoscopes and astrology fortunes. Go to a Chinese restaurant and after your meal the waiter will present you with fortune cookies.

These are all ways in which we tell ourselves that we might be able to foresee something in our future. In Lyra's case, the alethiometer actually does seem to tell truths about things—past, present, and future. But it only tells truths because Lyra's mind is attuned to knowing how to make it work. Lyra is the ultimate fortune teller, in today's parlance. She is connected to the cosmic consciousness we've described in detail earlier in this book; she's able to communicate with the universe and find truth. She interprets her alethiometer using techniques espoused by spirituals and shamans through the centuries, by books such as the I Ching, which is mentioned in *His Dark Materials* and described in the next chapter.

Another device, the Lodestone Resonator, plays an important role in *The Amber Spyglass*. We first witness the Lodestone Resonator in action when Lady Salmakia is watching the dragonfly spies hatch from a cocoon and Chevalier Tialys is sending a spy message to Lord Roke. Instantly, Tialys gets a response from Lord Roke (*The Amber Spyglass*, page 145).

He later tells Lyra that he talks to Lord Roke through the Lodestone Resonator. Lyra notes that the communications device ". . . looked like a short length of pencil made of dull gray-black stone, resting on a stand of wood, and the Chevalier swept a tiny bow like a violinist's across the end while he pressed his fingers at various points along the surface." Tialys uses miniature headphones to hear responses; the headphones are miniature, of course, because Tialys is a miniature man. He tells Lyra that the device works using something called quantum entanglement. No matter how far apart two particles are from each other, if something happens to one of them, then it happens to the other one instantaneously. This is done using a lodestone and "entangling all its particles, and then splitting it in two so that both parts resonate together" (*The Amber Spyglass*, page 175).

A lodestone is a natural magnet made of a type of iron called magnetite. The magnetite becomes magnetic if it's exposed to a magnetic field that is stronger than Earth's magnetic field. If lightning strikes magnetite, the iron's particles align in such a way that they produce a magnetic field.

Do you remember when Lyra suggests that the Lodestone Resonator reminds her of the alethiometer? This is because both act like compasses. In fact, some of the first compasses ever made, some 2,000 years ago, consisted of lodestone.

Because the lodestone is magnetic, in the real world a Lodestone Resonator would create electromagnetic waves, which are like long, rippling radio waves. Basically, the Resonator would operate as a radio transmitter, sending signals at the speed of light. Is it conceivable that a radio transmitter can broadcast signals from our world to another one? It seems highly unlikely.

The speed of light, as mentioned earlier, is 186,000 miles per second. It takes a radio about 0.016th of a second to send a transmission from New York City to London, which is about 3,000 miles across the Atlantic Ocean. The radio transmission happens so quickly that the listener doesn't notice any delay whatsoever.

However, the same radio transmission from New York City to the moon would take much longer. Consider that the moon is 250,000 miles away. Let's do some simple arithmetic:

$$3,000 \text{ miles} / 0.016 \text{ second} = 250,000 \text{ miles} / \times$$
$$3,000 \times = (250,000)(0.016)$$
$$3,000 \times = 4,000$$
$$\times = 4,000 / 3,000$$
$$\times = 1.33 \text{ seconds}$$

So if you want to talk to someone on the moon, there will be a 1.33 second delay from the time you talk to the time they hear you, and vice versa. If you say, "Hey, buddy, whatcha doin'?" and your pal responds, "Nothin' much, bongo," you won't hear him say "bongo" for approximately 2.6 seconds. That's a bit of a delay when you're trying to talk about something that matters, such as Gallivespian spying.

The Lodestone Resonator, however, doesn't take this long to transmit messages. Rather, the messages are communicated instantly across worlds. There is absolutely no delay. The device relies on quantum entanglement.

Most simply put, quantum entanglement in the real world means that after two things interact, they always know what's happening with each other. Even when far apart—say, worlds apart—the two things still know instantaneously, just as with a Lodestone Resonator, what is happening at the other end.

Tiny things such as electrons and other particles have waves associated with them. When waves of two quantum particles get tangled, it's called quantum entanglement. If the two quantum particles move far apart, their waves stretch and maintain communication between them, even if the particles are on opposite sides of the universe. Because we don't know about our parallel universes—not yet—it's unclear how this might work across universes.

If one atom is split to produce two particles that are spinning in opposite directions, then those two particles are said to be entangled. If one is horizontally polarized, the other might be vertically polarized.

Experiments have actually shown that two particles with different polarizations can become entangled on opposite sides of a room. When an atom is split and produces two photons that spin in different directions and with different polarizations, those two photons become entangled.

Photons are spin-one quantum particles traveling at the speed of light, and each photon spins in one direction of motion. If you could see a photon as it approached you, it might appear to be right- or left-handed, depending on the spin. Notice that we're talking about spin as if the photon is a particle.

As for polarization, it has to do with the wavelike property of light, and it is related to the particle-like property of the photon's spin. According to Maxwell's equations, which we need not explore in depth in this book, a light wave's magnetic and electric fields oscillate at right angles to the direction in which the light is traveling. A photon's polarization refers to the direction in which its electric field is oscillating. Photons can be polarized in many directions, but if a polarizing filter is used (think about sunglasses), the light can be forced into oscillating in specific directions. If a filter is slanted in a particular direction, then the polarization of the photons is slanted in a particular direction.

Using computers to make things happen, scientists change one photon and notice that the other photon does the same thing. For example, a photon flies through a vertical slit and becomes horizontally polarized, and instantly the other photon becomes horizontally polarized.

Using quantum entanglement in 2002, Australian scientists shifted an entire laser beam a distance of one meter. They started with two laser beams, each containing billions of photons that were entangled with photons from the other beam. They poked one laser beam, and all of its photons "jiggled"; and as the photons in the first beam jiggled, the photons in the second beam jiggled, too. Even stranger, when the information about jiggling went from one set of photons to the other set, the entire first laser beam disappeared. It was as if the first laser beam had teleported to a distance one meter away: just like on *Star Trek*.

According to *Nature* magazine in 2001, "a pair of quantum particles can exist in entangled superposition, a mixture of states that resolves only when some physical property such as spin or polarization is measured. Quantum entanglement is a fundamental requirement for quantum computing. . . . Using a new method of generating entanglement, an entangled state involving two macroscopic objects, each consisting of a cesium gas sample containing about 10^{12} atoms, has now been created."[105] This work was done by Eugene Polzik at the University of Aarhus's Quantum Optics Center in Denmark. Basically, his team used an infrared beam of light to make a cloud of one trillion atoms of cesium gas assume the quantum spin of another cesium cloud.[106] What this means is that scientists as far back as 2001 were already making larger objects become entangled, and this entanglement, existing only for 0.5 milliseconds, gave scientists hope that quantum computers and teleportation would someday exist.

Further, says the *Christian Science Monitor*, scientists in Denmark "have entangled two large clusters of atoms in neighboring containers. The feat, the team says, represents the first demonstration of entanglement between separated, large clusters of atoms, at room temperature, and for relatively long periods of time."[107] Earlier, scientists at the National Institute of Standards and Technology in Boulder, Colorado, had entangled four atoms.

At the end of 2004, as I write this book, scientists have used entangled photons to transfer money and have commercial hardware to support quantum cryptography.[108] The Swiss company ID Quantique and the American company MagiQ are marketing

105. "Quantum Entanglement: Going Large." *Nature*, September 27, 2001, http://www.nature.com/nature/links/010927/010927-2.html.
106. B. Julsgaard, A. Kozhekin, and E. S. Polzik, "Experimental Long-Lived Entanglement of Two Macroscopic Quantum Objects." *Nature*, Issue 413, 2001, pp. 400–403.
107. Peter N. Spotts, "Spooky Action at a Distance." *The Christian Science Monitor*, October 4, 2001. http://www.csmonitor.com/2001/1004/p15sl-stss.html.
108. Mark Buchanan, "Quantum Tricks that Read Your Thoughts." *New Scientist*, December 4, 2004. http://www.newscientist.com/channel/fundamentals/quantum-world/.

quantum cryptography, with most customers coming from the military ranks and other government organizations. Quantum computing, in very general terms, uses the various states of photons to represent bits of data. It works along short distances of fiber optic cable, but scientists hope that quantum repeaters can be used someday to enable transfer of quantum-based computer data along much longer distances.

Entanglement has yet to be used for quantum cryptography, though it has been used to transfer money. In 2004, the Bank Austria Creditanstalt used a system developed by the ARC Seibersdorf Research company to transfer electronic funds from Vienna City Hall. The fiber optic cable ran 1.5 kilometers between the two buildings.

Also in 2004, Massachusetts company BBN Technologies created a computer network whose security was based on quantum cryptography. Funded by the Pentagon's Defense Advanced Research Projects Agency (DARPA), BBN Technologies' Quantum Net (Qnet) system uses six "quantum" servers and 10 kilometers of fiber optic cable.

The Lodestone Resonator is a possibility, though not for a long time. Whether it can work across the galaxies and from one parallel world to another is an unknown. Whether it can work using lodestone is another unknown. What is known, however, is that quantum entanglement is a real technology in the real world.

Another real technology used in *His Dark Materials* is the idea behind the spy dragonflies, which are mechanical insects. Our first encounter with a mechanical insect is in *The Golden Compass*, when Lyra's on a boat with an old tillerman. Pantalaimon is having a good time, cruising around as a seagull, when suddenly the daemon is attacked. A series of black fluttering objects strikes him, and Lyra notes that they are like flying beetles. They drone, they buzz, and they're murderous (*The Golden Compass*, page 153).

Later, Lyra examines one of the mechanical insects. It's the size of her thumb, has six clawed legs, and furiously beating wings. Farder Coram explains that it's a mechanical device operating on a clockwork. Inside the clock spring is a bad spirit that kills everything around it (*The Golden Compass*, page 154). They must keep the insect in a tight box, where its struggles will make the clockwork wind more tightly, increasing its potency and deadly power. The clock springs never run down, and the insects never "die" (*The Golden Compass*, page 156).

While the part about the bad spirit isn't based on anything that exists today, the mechanical insect itself is based on real technology.

At Vanderbilt University, scientists have been building mechanical insects for years. As far back as 1997 and 1998, Professors Ephrahim Garcia and Michael Goldfarb were developing tiny robotic insects under contract to DARPA. They equipped their insects with microelectromechanical systems, or MEMS, used "elasto-dynamic locomotion" and piezoelectric actuators to power the insects.[109]

As far back as 2001, scientists were working on robotic insects to flap through the thin atmosphere of Mars. This work, guided by team leader Robert Michelson at Georgia Tech Research Institute, was also funded by DARPA. Meanwhile, at the University of Cambridge in England, scientists were creating robotic insects based on analyses of the hawk moth.[110]

In April 2001, scientists at California company AeroVironment tested the flight of the world's first robotic insect. The company had been developing micro-spy planes for many years. Their

109. "Vanderbilt University Engineers Developing Robotic Insects," http://www.robotbooks.com/robot-insects.htm.
110. Leonard David, "Flapping Robotic Insects Could Extend Range of Rover Missions," http://www.space.com/scienceastronomy/solarsystem/mars flapper 011205-1.html.

earlier Black Widow, a six-inch-diameter black robotic insect plane, had been used by the United States military for spying missions over enemy lines.[111]

In 2002, NASA was funding research directed at building robotic insects to fly around Mars and collect data. Based on the entomology of insects, the robot versions hovered like helicopters and were called entomopters. University of Missouri professor Kakkattukuzhy Isaac said, "We are looking mainly at the dragonfly, the hummingbird and the fruit fly, but we are not trying to mimic one particular insect. Instead we are identifying the principles that enable insects to create such high lift . . ." The NASA project included scientists at Georgia Tech Research Institute, the University of Cambridge in England, and the Ohio Aerospace Institute.[112]

Michelson's entomopter, also known as a multimodal electromechanical insect, was awarded a patent in July 2000 for Georgia Tech Research Corporation. The entomopter is expected to do far more than roam around other planets (as if that weren't enough to do for a robotic insect). Other uses will be crawling around ventilation systems and through dangerous areas here on Earth. The basic parts of the entomopter are described at the *How Stuff Works* Web site,[113] and we'll summarize the ideas here:

The fuselage of the robotic insect houses the power source and the fuel tank. All other parts of the insect connect to the fuselage, which is like the hull of an airplane.

Made from a thin film, the wings of the robotic insect are coupled to the fuselage. The insect has two wings in the front

111. Chris Riley, "Robotic Insect Takes to the Air." *BBC News*, as reported at http://news.bbc.co.uk/1/hi/sci/tech/1270306.stm.

112. R. Colin Johnson, "Flying Robotic Insect Slated to Explore Mars." *EE Times*, http://www.eet.com/story/OEG20020114S0081.

113. Kevin Bonsor, "How Spy Flies Will Work," http://science.howstuffworks.com/spy-fly1.htm.

and two wings in the back, and each wing includes flexible veins for the required curve to generate lift. A reciprocating chemical muscle, or noncombustive engine, enables the wings to flap.

The robotic insect includes sensors, which enable it to look in all directions. And the insect may soon carry a tiny camera, as well as an olfactory sensor that will enable it to track odors back to their origins. These parts will help the insect operate as a spy, just as the robotic insects in *His Dark Materials* operate as spies.

Final components of the robotic insect include legs and feet, or surface locomotors.

In August 2003, MIT scientists created a robotic insect that walked on water. According to *BBC News*, scientists John "Bush and his collaborators, David Hu and Brian Chan, discovered that the secret to the water strider's locomotion is that it rows across the water without penetrating the surface. The rowing motion leaves a telltale vortex behind each foot, clearly visible on camera."[114] After figuring out how the real water strider made its way across the water, the scientists then created a robotic version of the insect.

In 2004, approximately 3,000 of the world's leading insect scientists attended the International Congress of Entomology in Brisbane to consider how to develop robotic insects.[115] And in 2004, Steve Zornetzer, NASA's director of information technologies, said that it's "just a matter of time before they fill a Mars spaceship with robotic insects that will explore the red planet in ways no one ever thought imaginable."[116] In Australia, scientists have created honeybee robots, which are tiny remotely controlled

114. Ivan Noble, "Robot Insect Walks on Water." *BBC News*, as reported at http://news.bbc.co.uk/1/hi/sci/tech/3126299.stm.

115. "Insect-Based Robots to Fly like Magic." *ABC News Online*, August 2004, as reported at http://www.abc.net.au/science/news/scitech/SciTechRepublish_1181486.htm.

116. Jonathan Gravenor, "Bee Robotics." January 2004, as reported at http://www.xposed.com/gadgets/bee robotics.aspx.

planes that function like honeybees. Computer software makes the bees fly through trees and over hills. And computer software is being developed that makes the bees think like insects as well.[117]

To really understand how robotic spies work, go to the *How Stuff Works* Web site. In his article (mentioned earlier), the author Kevin Bonsor explains that the U.S. Department of Defense is spending millions of dollars to develop micro air vehicles (MAVs), which are robotic insects equipped with tiny cameras. "One class of these MAVs," writes Bonsor, "is being designed to mimic the flying motions of certain insects, including flies, bees and dragonflies."[118]

There's one more section to this chapter, and it's also about flying machines. But these machines aren't based on insects. They're more like gigantic air balloons and airplanes. As our final section on "Weird Science, Part 1," let's take a brief look at the zeppelins and gyrocopters of *His Dark Materials*.

Balloons and airships are the two types of craft that are lighter than air. Both are called aerostats, and both rise into the air and stay there because they are so light. At first, the balloons rose using hot air, and later in World War II, propane burners enabled hot air balloons to stay aloft for long periods of time.

For more than a century, balloons and airships used hydrogen to provide lift, though for a while around 1917, helium was also used.

Basically, an airship is powered and can be controlled along a horizontal path; a balloon just rises into the air and floats with minor operator control. The balloon's horizontal direction is based on the wind.

When propulsion and horizontal control are added to a bal-

117. Ibid.
118. Kevin Bonsor, op. cit.

loon, it becomes a basic airship. This type of airship was first flown in France between 1852 and 1884. The word *dirigible* is from the French *dirigeable*, which is derived from *diriger*, to control or steer. Originally, the steerable lighter-than-air craft was termed a *ballon dirigeable*. Today, the French word for aircraft is *dirigeable*—without the *ballon*. Originally, the English term for the same aircraft was dirigible balloon, though today it's called simply a dirigible.

In the early twentieth century, the airship was available in a rigid framework and a pressure-rigid framework. Both were cylindrical, and both rose into the air using engine-driven propellers and gas. They were controlled by vertical rudders and horizontal elevators.

The rigid framework featured a skeleton with external fabric. Metal was not in use yet for aircraft. Bags of gas called ballonets were inside the framework. The pressure-rigid framework did not include a skeleton. In this type of aircraft, the shape of the fabric was maintained by the pressure of the gas filling the fabric (yes, much like a balloon).

It's the rigid framework that eventually became a zeppelin. Shortly after 1900, a cavalry officer from Württemberg, Ferdinand Adolf August Heinrich Graf von Zeppelin, perfected the aircraft. In 1863, Zeppelin had flown balloons in the United States. Of course, the rigid framework that Zeppelin perfected became known as a zeppelin, which is a trademarked name for aircraft made exclusively by the company Luftshiffbau Zeppelin G.m.b.H. or other companies with licenses. The use of the word *zeppelin* in *His Dark Materials* is slightly off-kilter, then, as it references a generic class of aircraft. Of course, *His Dark Materials* takes place in parallel worlds, so perhaps on another world a zeppelin accurately refers to a similar type of aircraft that doesn't belong to a specific company.

From 1915 through 1918, the British navy used more than

two hundred pressure-rigid zeppelins. Other countries using zeppelins during this period included France, Italy, Germany, and the United States.

The last rigid zeppelin was built in the 1930s, though pressure-rigid zeppelins are still being used. Today, the pressure-rigid zeppelins are known as blimps.

The modern blimp has specific parts that enable it to fly through the air under human control. For example, the envelope is the fabric containing the helium gas. It is shaped like a cigar.

Nose cone battens give the front of the blimp—or the nose—an aerodynamic shape. These are supports that stiffen the nose of the blimp so it won't get damaged.

A blimp has two ballonets, one in the front, one in the back. Ballonets are the bags of air inside the envelope, and to make the blimp go up and down, the bags are deflated and inflated with air.

The envelope also contains two catenary curtains, which are made from fabric. The curtains help support the blimp and maintain its shape, and are attached to the envelope with suspension cables.

The blimp has two turbo-propeller airplane engines that use gas fuel. The engines enable the blimp to travel up to seventy miles per hour.

Air scoops push the exhaust air from the propellers into the ballonets, so the pilots can fill the ballonets during the flight. Four air valves let the pilots vent air from the blimp.

Passengers and crew sit in the gondola of the blimp. Today's blimp may hold up to fourteen people.

So now you basically know what a zeppelin is—think of the Goodyear Blimp and you're on the right track. So what's a gyrocopter?

The short answer is that a gyrocopter is like a mini-helicopter. The autogiro, which is also called a gyrocopter, gyroplane, or windmill plane, was invented by Don Juan de la Cierva in Spain and made its first flight in January of 1923. In the 1930s and 1940s, the U.S. postal service used gyrocopters to deliver mail in Washington, D.C., Chicago, Los Angeles, Philadelphia, and New Orleans.

Like helicopters, gyrocopters can take off and land vertically. But the two are different. For example, the gyrocopter doesn't go particularly fast or for long distances. It has an airplane-like propeller to move it forward, and it has a helicopter-like rotor to move it vertically.

It's true that the helicopter and gyrocopter seem somewhat similar. Both have rotors and motors. However, the airplane propeller of the gyrocopter provides a main difference. This difference is in the way the lift is powered.

The gyrocopter's lift is powered by forward propulsion using the propeller, which creates a wind that passes through the rotors and lifts the craft. While a motor powers the propeller, only the wind powers the rotor. In a helicopter, a motor powers both the movement forward and the lift.

Because of the differences in how it is powered, the gyrocopter uses less fuel: The motor powers the propulsion but not the lift, hence requiring less fuel than the helicopter's motor.

Of course, this factor also means that the gyrocopter doesn't hover the way helicopters hover. Instead, the gyrocopter must be moving forward to maintain lift. The helicopter does not need forward motion to maintain lift, so it can hover.

There are a few other differences, but you get the idea: The gyrocopter is like a mini-helicopter, slightly different but very similar.

Now let's move into our last chapter, "Weird Science, Part 2." Here we'll whip through some final bits from *His Dark Materials,* and we'll touch on the I Ching and shamanism.

WEIRD SCIENCE, PART 2

Welcome to the final chapter of this book. We've made it through a lot of subjects: consciousness, Dust, dark matter, dark energy, the big bang, astronomy, angels, God, heaven, hell, the afterlife, witches, daemons and souls, parallel worlds, specters, vampires, night ghasts, zombies, the Aurora Borealis, the alethiometer, the Lodestone Resonator and quantum entanglement, robotic insects, zeppelins, and gyrocopters. And I'm probably leaving a few subjects out . . .

In this, our last chapter, we tie up the final tidbits of weird science related to *His Dark Materials*. These tidbits aren't as thrilling as the chapters about Dust, consciousness, heaven, hell, and souls—to name only a few sections in the Front Matter of this book. And that's why I called this part of the book the Back Matter. We need to include these tidbits, but we don't need to put them up front.

So hold on, here we go: our final chapter!

First, we're going to journey back a little and remember that Dust is dark matter, and that dark matter is also known in *His Dark Materials* as shadow particles and cosmic consciousness. In

The Subtle Knife, Mary Malone tells Lyra that she uses the I Ching to communicate with the shadows or Dust aka dark matter. The Chinese I Ching, she says, is a form of fortune-telling (*The Subtle Knife*, pages 88–91).

We also learn that Mary Malone has studied an I Ching book for many years and that Lyra knows the Dust can speak to human beings using the I Ching symbols. In fact, Malone uses the I Ching to decipher the meanings of clues she receives about the parallel worlds (*The Amber Spyglass*, pages 80–82). She continues to use the I Ching for advice, and it continues to give her answers.

As you might have guessed, the I Ching is real. It's also called *The Book of Changes* or the Chou I, and it was developed in China a long time ago. The I Ching was studied by the Confucians during the last period of the Chou era, and as such, was one of the few books that the Chinese government authorized. In 140 B.C., all non-Confucian texts were excluded from the imperial academy, making the I Ching doctrine. And in fact, the imperial academy established a chair of study for the I Ching, which has lasted throughout Chinese history.

Over time, *The Book of Changes* or I Ching rose to a level far beyond that of a scholarly text. According to authorities on the I Ching, it became a volume of "sacred scriptures inspired by divine revelation. The reason seems to lie in the concentration of divine as well as temporal power in the person of the emperor, in China as well as in other oriental societies. The emperor was not only the sole source of political decisions, he was also the Son of Heaven, the representative of the deity among men . . ."[119] Note the similarity to the idea of the alethiometer,

---

119. Hellmut Wilhelm and Richard Wilhelm, *Understanding the I Ching: The Wilhelm Lectures on the Book of Changes*. Princeton, NJ: Princeton University Press, 1995, page 5. According to Princeton University Press, Richard Wilhelm was the West's foremost translator of the I Ching.

which requires the concentration of the divine, in this case Dust or dark matter, the cosmic consciousness, as well as the temporal power of Lyra, who operates somewhat as a representative of the cosmic consciousness among humans. What Lyra can do with the alethiometer, Mary attempts to do with the I Ching. Both communicate with the cosmic consciousness—which is the divine in *His Dark Materials*—using sacred instruments of focus.

Corresponding closely to the idea of cosmic consciousness in the trilogy of novels, the I Ching views the universe as a natural whole in which change is continual yet connected. Human nature and destiny are closely aligned with universal principles. By studying the I Ching, people hope to guide their activities and thoughts, their courses of action, within the larger context of harmonious interactions among other people, nature, and the entire cosmos.

The I Ching has symbols on it in the form of sixty-four hexagrams, each consisting of six horizontal lines. While some of these lines are solid, others have gaps in the middle. Each hexagram is made of a pair of three symbols, which are called trigrams, and each hexagram has a name. Each trigram has a special meaning, and to learn the meanings, a person studies the I Ching, which interprets all the meanings in a series of commentaries. Basically, each hexagram symbolizes particular situations, and the hexagram's name refers to these situations, which, in turn, are described in the I Ching. It's very similar to Lyra's use of the alethiometer: She uses the needles of the alethiometer and the corresponding symbols to interpret events; and with the I Ching, Mary Malone uses the hexagram symbols to interpret events.

In the I Ching are images about a person's primary needs, his social life, his character traits, and so forth. For example, there are images to represent obstacles, oppression, abundance, the mistakes of youth; a marrying girl, friendship, seeking love, finding love, family, peace, conflict, war; modesty, innocence, truth, enthusiasm; joy, arousal, and gentleness.

Consulting the I Ching is much like consulting the alethiometer or the ouija board. First you think of a question about something you intend to do. The question should go far beyond the type of question that we answer with ouija board yes and no movements. For example, you wouldn't want to ask a question like "Will it rain today?" You want to think of a question that's more complex, such as the questions Mary Malone asks of the I Ching: "Should I be here doing this, or should I go somewhere else and keep searching?" In her case, the I Ching responds, "Keeping still, see that restlessness dissolves; then, beyond the tumult, one can perceive the great laws." And it continues with more detailed advice (*The Amber Spyglass*, page 124).

A common way of picking out an initial hexagram as you concentrate on your question is to toss three coins. You don't need to use ancient Chinese coins; any three coins will do. The head side of the coin stands for yang, and the tail side stands for yin.

In short, yin and yang are the primal opposing elements found in the universe, with yin being the absence of yang rather than its opposite. Yin and yang aren't analogous to good and evil, or vice versa; rather, they are in constant harmony, balancing each other. For example, yin might refer to the moon and represent feminine nature, while yang might refer to the sun and represent masculine nature. Yin might refer to the stillness of a traffic light, while the actual traffic might be associated with yang.

So you toss the three coins and come up with a yin-yang combination related to your question. For a yin-sided coin, assign two points, and for a yang-sided coin, assign three points. This will enable you to generate the six lines of the initial hexagram. After you toss the three coins, add up their yin-yang values. For example, if all three coins land on yang sides, the total value is nine; if two coins land on yang sides while one lands on yin, your total value is eight. Based on the total value, draw the first line of your initial hexagram. This first line will be the bottom-most line of the hexagram.

For a six, draw a line that looks like this:

▬▬▬ X ▬▬▬

For a seven, draw a line that looks like this:

▬▬▬▬▬▬▬

For an eight, draw a line that looks like this:

▬▬▬   ▬▬▬

For a nine, draw a line that looks like this:

▬▬▬ o ▬▬▬

It's a bit complicated, because as you see, some of the lines have tiny X's and O's in the middle. The line corresponding to the value of six has an X and refers to a "moving" yin line, while the nine refers to a "moving" yang line. For simplicity's sake—or until you become expert—you might want to change the moving yin line to a yang and change the moving yang to a yin.

Now toss the three coins again, add their yin-yang values, and draw the next line over the first line. Repeat the process until you have a stack of six lines.

Suppose your lines end up looking like this:

Flip through your copy of the I Ching and locate the hexagram that looks like your stack of lines. The hexagram is number 8, meaning a union of things, holding something together.

Now read the interpretation in the I Ching. The judgment

section of the interpretation is: "Holding together brings good fortune. Inquire of the oracle once again whether you possess sublimity, constancy, and perseverance; then there is no blame. Those who are uncertain gradually join. Whoever comes too late meets with misfortune."[120] One thing you notice right away is that you must ask the oracle, or the I Ching, if you possess sublimity, constancy, and perseverance. Based on that answer, you can then continue the interpretation of the initial hexagram number 8.

We'll do one more example, and then shift the topic to shamanism, which is another spiritual subject of *His Dark Materials* that relates directly to the cosmic consciousness. In this final example, I think the question, "Will my readers like this book?" I toss the three coins, calculate the values, draw my six lines. I end up with these six lines:

This corresponds to hexagram 9, called "the taming power of the small." According to the I Ching, hexagram 9 means "the taming power of the small has success. Dense clouds, no rain from our western region."[121] The interpretation indicates that I

120. Richard Wilhelm and Cary F. Baynes, *The I Ching or Book of Changes*. Princeton, NJ: Princeton University Press, 1977, p. 56; original copyright 1950 by Bollingen Foundation, Inc., New York.
121. Ibid., pp. 40–41.

need "firm determination within and gentleness and adaptability in external relations" and that I must "return to the way suited to [my] situation, where [I am] free to advance or retreat."[122] I take this to mean that I should write books that truly drive me and that, while many people will like this particular book, it won't become a *New York Times* bestseller.[123] But this is just my reflection upon what I see in the I Ching, based on my six random tosses of the three coins.

As mentioned, shamanism is closely related to the ideas behind the alethiometer and the I Ching; all three hinge on the notion of cosmic consciousness, the unity of the universe. We first encounter shamanism in the beginning of *The Golden Compass*, when Lord Asriel shows Stanislaus Grumman's head to the scholars. He explains that the head is scalped in a way that reminds him of a method used by the Tartars. The hole in the top of Grumman's head is known as trepanning (*The Golden Compass*, page 25).

Later, we learn that the Tartars have been drilling holes into people's heads for thousands of years (*The Golden Compass*, page 228) and that Grumman was a shaman (*The Subtle Knife*, page 209). When we encounter Grumman as a live man, he explains that he knows how to make ointments from bloodmoss and he knows how to enter deep trances to learn things about spirits of the world (*The Subtle Knife*, page 215).

A shaman is a medicine man or witch doctor, a sorcerer or magician. He possesses magical-religious powers and usually is in charge of the well-being of his community.

While shamanism has existed throughout many cultures and thousands of centuries, it is primarily found in Siberia and

122. Ibid.
123. No surprises here!

Central Asia. The word *shamani* is derived from the Russian evolution of the Tungusic word *saman*. In Central and Northern Asia, people rely on shamans for magical-religious purposes, and in many tribes, priests confer with their shamans before making sacred decisions. Shamanism refers to the techniques used to create ecstasy; and ecstasy is supposedly the ultimate religious experience: It is the deep trance to which Grumman refers.

In the Arctic and Siberia, many people are hunters, fishers, and herdsmen. Many are nomads, at least to some extent. Despite differences in language and ethnicity, they share a belief in an all-powerful creator. This is true for the Turko-Tatars, Chukchee, Tungus, and others. It might be the Turko-Tatars from which Pullman derived his Tartars.

The roots of the Tatars are directly connected to Turkic tribes. The first Turks came from Asia to Eastern Europe in approximately the fourth century. They used a common name: the Huns, which in Turkic is Hen or Sen.

King of the Huns from 433 through 453 A.D., Attila was one of the most notorious barbarians in all of history. Of distant Mongol ancestry, Attila ravaged the European continent, was known as the Scourge of God, and raged against the Teutonic tribespeople as well as the Romans. Under Attila's rule, the Huns conquered everything from the Rhine River to the north of the Black Sea and as far as the Caspian Sea. From there, they attacked the Roman Empire's capitals of Constantinople in the east and Ravenna in the west.

The Tatars, or Tartars in Pullman's world, did indeed practice shamanism. The Arctic, Siberian, and Central Asian religions enabled shamanism to reach its most advanced integration into the ordinary, daily lives of people. In fact, some scholars think that shamanism originated in the Arctic. It's believed that the inhabitants of polar regions exhibited pronounced nervous instabilities

due to the extreme cold, long nights, solitude, and lack of vita-
mins. Hence, the Arctic people, according to this theory, developed mental illnesses known primarily as Arctic hysteria, which
actually might have been the shaman's trance. In fact, it's been
written that the "only difference between a shaman and an
epileptic is that the latter cannot deliberately enter into a
trance."[124] Further, the Arctic shaman's trances generally ended
with an epileptic trance, during which the people believed the
shaman's soul left his body and traveled through the sky into the
vast cosmic wonderland.

If a child was sick, the Tatar people might have called upon
the shaman for help, and he would have held a séance to try to
bring back the soul of the child. The Tatar shaman's séance
lasted up to six hours and in it, the shaman went on an ecstatic
journey (or trance) to other lands, where he searched for the sick
child's undamaged soul and for a remedy to the illness. In the extreme northeast region of Siberia, the Chukchee shaman simu-
lated trances for fifteen minutes or so, during which he asked the
spirits to help the child.

Whatever aid he's trying to offer his people, the shaman basically travels from one cosmic region to another for advice and
help. He knows how to communicate on the cosmic plane, or via
the cosmic consciousness, just as the shaman does in *His Dark
Materials*. The difference perhaps is that the real shaman thinks
of the universe as having three cosmic dimensions: earth, sky,
and underworld; and in *His Dark Materials*, the universes share
one cosmic consciousness through the Dust or dark matter.

The Turko-Tatars thought the sky was a tent, with the Milky
Way being a seam and the stars being holes in the tent's fabric.
Every now and then, the gods opened the tent to look at the peo-

124. Mircea Eliade, *Shamanism: Archaic Techniques of Ecstasy*. Princeton, NJ: Princeton
University Press, 1964, p. 24.

ple rambling around on the Earth. In the middle of the sky was the Pole Star that served as a stake to hold up the tent. The Siberian Tatars called it the Solar Pillar. According to the Chukchee, the shaman communicates with the sky by taking the road through the Pole Star, which is a hole connecting the three cosmic dimensions. The Buryat people thought their shaman opened the road to the sky (via the Pole Star) just as easily as a person opens a door.

As for trepanning, the procedure used by the shamans in *His Dark Materials*, it is a real procedure. It's a process by which a hole is cut in the skull. Medically, it might be used to relieve pressure on the brain, to remove a blood clot in the brain, or to lift a fracture from the skull bone. Trepanning is also called trepanation or trephination, which is derived from the Greek term *trypanon* meaning borer.

Evidence of trepanning dates as far back as four thousand years, when the Indians of Peru performed the operation. In fact, trepanning may have been used by people since prehistory; skulls with precisely drilled holes in them have been found in many archaeological digs throughout the world.

In our real world, primitive people believed in evil spirits and other supernatural forces. Shamanism was widespread. Trepanning may have been used to open the shaman's mind to the cosmic consciousness, let the forces of good spirits inside his head, and let the evil spirits out of his head. By forcing bad spirits from the head, the shaman might be clear of insanity and other mental deficiencies that could impede his ability to help the tribe.

To drill a trepanning hole, a surgeon cuts the scalp over the skull and pulls back a flap of skin. He then bores a hole into the skull bone using a saw or a trephine (a type of saw) with a drill. He then removes a circle of bone that's about the size of a nickel. Don't try it at home!

GLOSSARY

Adamant Tower. Lord Asriel's headquarters in the basalt fortress.

Aesahaettr. The name used for the subtle knife by the cliff ghasts.

Alethiometer. A truth-telling device that looks like a compass. Only six alethiometers have ever been made. The alethiometer has thirty-six pictures around its dial, and it has three hands, three winding wheels, and a compass-like needle.

Anbaric. Electricity; in Lyra's world, an energy source and charge. Anbarology is the study of anbaric forces.

Angels. Also called the *bene elim* and the *Watchers*, they look like humans with wings but they're created from Dust. The angels are ancient beings, and most are extremely kind and intelligent.

Arc. An evenly curved arch of Northern Lights with a smooth lower edge.

Armored Bears. Also called the Panserborne, they are a form of polar bear without daemons. The armored bears make and wear armor, hence their name. They also communicate with humans and can always be relied upon if they give their word to do something.

Aurora Borealis. Another name for the Northern Lights, it is created by the interactions among the solar wind, the Earth's magnetosphere, and the upper atmosphere. In the southern hemisphere, the phenomenon is called the Aurora Australis.

Authority. The first angel, made out of Dust, the Authority pretended to be the creator. His regent, Metatron, assumed most of his power and control over humans.

Balthamos. The angel companion of Baruch, a lower angel who rebelled against the Authority.

Band. Not as even as an arc of Northern Lights, with kinks and folds on the lower edge.

Baruch. The angel companion of Balthamos, a lower angel who was a human in Will's world about four thousand years ago.

Baryonic Matter. A baryon is a small particle, like a neutron or proton, that is a strongly interacting particle. The type of matter we find on Earth, baryonic matter makes up only a small portion of the total matter in the universe. There's far more dark matter than baryonic matter.

Big Bang. The original explosion that created our universe approximately fourteen billion years ago. Evidence of the Big Bang comes from three experimental proofs: cosmic background microwave radiation, nucleosynthesis of the elements, and the redshift of the galaxies.

Black Hole. An object in outer space that has an escape velocity equal to the speed of light. It is thought by most scientists today that nothing can escape from a black hole because the speed of light is the maximum velocity in the universe. The black hole has tremendous density, with a mass of approximately four billion of our suns. It eats gaseous matter at the rate of a million suns per year.

Bloodmoss. Herbs that stop bleeding and help wounds heal.

Brane. A membrane, which can be in any dimension from one to eleven. A cross section of an eleven-dimension brane is a ten-dimensional string.

Brown Dwarfs. Stars with a mass less than eight percent of the sun's mass, brown dwarfs are failed stars that glow for a while after they are formed. Scientists have no evidence that the galaxy has enough brown dwarfs to account for the dark matter.

Causal Determinism. Proposed by Isaac Newton, causal determinism means that, given the laws of motion and the facts about where objects are before they move and how fast they're moving, we can predict the exact locations of the objects.

Chandra X-Ray Telescope. A telescope in outer space that scans the universe for X-ray emissions from neutron stars, black holes, and other objects.

Cittàgazze. A city inhabited by specters that suck the life out of adults but leave children alone. Will and Lyra first meet in Cittàgazze, and it's on a parallel world different from either of their home worlds.

Cliff Ghasts. Stinking mythological-type creatures who attack people from cliffs.

Cold Dark Matter. Particles that are heavier than neutrinos and that move slowly, and hence might have formed the clusters of galaxies. Included among the cold dark matter candidates are the axions (named after a common detergent), photinos, zinos, and higgsinos. These are collectively known as super particles. Axions, for example, are very light, neutral particles that interact with tiny forces.

Coma Cluster. Collection of thousands of galaxies that are approximately 370 million light years from Earth, the Coma Cluster moves so quickly that, as far back as the 1930s, astronomers began suspecting the existence of invisible (dark) matter that might be binding them together.

Copenhagen School. An object exists in all possible states before we observe it. For example, a cat in a box may be dead or alive, but as soon as we observe the cat, we know which state it is in. Initiated by Niels Bohr, the Copenhagen School says that we must observe something to know what state it's really in.

Corona. A form of Northern Lights that has rayed arcs and bands, appearing like a sunburst blooming from the Earth.

Cosmic Consciousness. An all-knowing understanding of the universe.

Cosmic Microwave Background Radiation. Circulating through the universe, this radiation was left over after the Big Bang. The temperature of cosmic microwave background radiation is 2.7 degrees above absolute zero.

Cosmic String. Some scientists believe that remnants of the Big

Bang exist as huge cosmic strings of pure energy that are as big as galaxies.

Cosmos. The universe.

Daemons. These are analogous to souls and are made of the cosmic Dust or dark matter. They are intimately involved with a human's personality. When someone is a child, his daemon can change shape, and often does change shape as events dictate. As soon as a child reaches puberty, his daemon assumes its final form. All shapes and forms of daemons are animal in nature. Typically, the daemon is the opposite sex from its human; so Lyra's daemon is male and Lord Asriel's daemon is female. While witches can remain far apart from their daemons for short periods, humans and their daemons must remain close together; otherwise both experience great longing and pain.

Dark Energy. The energy in empty outer space, dark energy basically exists in proportion to the volume of the universe. Scientists have found that approximately 70 percent of the matter and energy in the entire universe is actually dark energy.

Dark Matter. In *His Dark Materials*, dark matter is the same as Dust, shadow particles, and cosmic consciousness, and souls, angels, and God are all made from it. In our world, dark matter is invisible, has very small weight, and does not interact with light. Scientists believe that dark matter makes up approximately 25 percent of the matter and energy in the entire universe. String theory indicates that dark matter may consist of subatomic particles, such as the neutrino.

Dimension. We ordinarily think of our universe in terms of three dimensions of space: length, width, and height; and one dimension of time. The math behind string theory and brane theory requires ten/eleven dimensions; and it's thought that we don't perceive the dimensions beyond the four of spacetime because they're curled up.

Dualism. Initially proposed by Descartes, this famous theory divides the world into two realms: the domain of science and matter (materialism) and the domain of mind and religion.

Dust. A force of nature that settles on people as they grow from children into adulthood. The Church hates the Dust, which is also referred to as Rusakov particles. Dust is the same as dark matter, which is the same as shadow particles, which, in turn, is the same as cosmic consciousness. Dust seems to bind the many parallel worlds; Dust forms the angels, the souls of the characters, and even God.

Einstein-Rosen Bridge. When two black-hole solutions are joined, they form a wormhole called an Einstein-Rosen Bridge. This is often used to describe spacetime as it exists near the center of a black hole.

Electromagnetism. Made up of tiny waves, this force provides light, radio, laser beams, television, and everything else that's driven by electrical power. An electromagnetic force includes both electricity and magnetism. When electricity and magnetism vibrate together, they create a wave, and it's this wave that describes light, radio, laser beams, television, and so forth. This is one of the four fundamental forces of the universe.

Epiphenomenalism. This theory hypothesizes that consciousness is a series of properties of the brain, which is composed of matter. Epiphenomenalism basically attempts to describe how consciousness might be derived from matter.

Event Horizon. This is a point of no return surrounding a black hole. Once you reach the event horizon, there's no turning back; you'll be sucked into the black hole.

Experimental Theology. In Lyra's world a serious field of study, in which theologians learn about the four fundamental forces of gravity, electromagnetism, weak nuclear force, and strong nuclear force; anbaromagnetic charges; and Dust.

Gaia. The whole of our living planet, named after the Greek Goddess of the Earth.

Galaxy. A collection of hundreds of billions of stars. Earth is in the Milky Way galaxy, which has up to 400 billion stars and their planets, as well as thousands of nebulae and clusters. The diameter of the Milky Way is approximately 100,000 light years.

Gallivespians. As tiny as human hands and as slender as dragon-flies, these people are fiercely independent and serve as spies.

Ghosts. In *The Amber Spyglass*, we encounter the ghosts of all dead people and the land of no return, where death prevails over a bleak landscape. These ghosts in the world of the dead are not the same as the specters that eat people in the world of Cittàgazze. Rather, these ghosts are distinct beings that are with people throughout life. A living person can even talk to his death.

Gravity. Holds the sun together and ensures that planets orbit around it. Without gravity, all the stars would explode and the planets would disintegrate. This is one of the four fundamental forces of the universe.

Gyrocopters. A type of helicopter used in Lyra's world.

Harpies. In Greek mythology, foul birds with the heads and breasts of human women. Just as they are in *His Dark Materials*, harpies had nasty claws and huge wings. They came from the river Styx and they smelled like rotting death.

Hot Dark Matter. A type of dark matter that might move extremely fast, near the speed of light, through outer space. Neutrinos, which are extremely light and chargeless, are categorized by many scientists as a form of hot dark matter.

Hyperspace. Refers to the dimensions higher than four. According to string and brane theory, there are ten/eleven hyperspace dimensions.

I Ching. Also known as *The Book of Changes* and the Chou I, this oracle-type text was developed in China a long time ago. It helps truthseekers predict future events and make important decisions.

Light Speed. 300,000 kilometers per second, or 186,000 miles per second.

Light Year. Distance light travels in one year, which is approximately 5.88 trillion miles. The Milky Way galaxy, in which Earth exists, is approximately 100,000 light years across.

Locality. Einstein's theory of relativity suggested that all interactions between objects in spacetime must be local: Objects travel one bit at a time with a finite velocity. This idea is known as locality.

Lodestone. Magnetic pieces of rock.

Lodestone Resonator. Used by the Gallivespians to communicate across far distances, this is a small block of stone.

MACHO. Massive Compact Halo Object; some people believe they might make up some portion of dark matter. MACHOs are the halos surrounding galaxies and have approximately half of the sun's mass.

Magnetic Field. Magnetic objects produce invisible lines, or fields, of force between their poles. The Earth has two poles, and magnetic lines/fields extend between them.

Magnetosphere. Region of outer space where a planet's magnetic field dominates the effects of the solar winds. Charged particles that become trapped on the magnetic lines extend between the North and South Poles form Earth's magnetosphere. This magnetosphere extends into outer space from fifty to 37,280 miles on the side of Earth facing the sun. On the other side of the planet, the magnetosphere extends approximately 186,500 miles into outer space.

Many-Worlds Theory. Quantum-based theory that suggests all possible universes can exist simultaneously.

Material Monism. A theory suggesting that everything in the universe, including our minds and consciousness, is composed of matter. Energy and force fields are intimately connected to matter, so they're included in this theory as well.

Material Realism. A theory that has five principles: causal determinism, strong objectivity, locality, material monism, and epiphenomenalism.

Membrane. Also called a brane, this is a surface that exists in any number of dimensions. Scientists view strings as a one-dimension membrane.

Monistic Idealism. The opposite of material realism, this theory suggests that we have a universal or cosmic consciousness, much in line with the philosophies of *His Dark Materials*.

Mrs. Coulter. No book about *His Dark Materials* can be complete without mentioning Mrs. Coulter (aka Cutter), the beautiful, strange, socialite mother of Lyra; the lover of Asriel; sometimes evil, sometimes seen in a more positive light. Her monkey daemon plays a big role in the books, too.

M-Theory. Existing in eleven-dimension spacetime, this is a type of string theory. Scientists postulate that M-Theory can be reduced to ten dimensions, which is why I write ten/eleven dimensions throughout this book when referring to superstring theory, branes, and possibilities for parallel worlds. Supposedly, there are five ways to reduce the eleven dimensions to ten, yielding a total of five current superstring theories. As of January 2005, as I finished writing this book, the most current information suggested that all five superstring theories may actually be one overall theory.

Multiverse. Shorthand for multiple universes. Scientists believe that an infinite number of parallel universes exist, possibly all split off from one another. In M-Theory, it's thought that these universes connect or collide with one another using membranes.

Naptha. In Lyra's world, this is a pre-anbaric form of energy.

Neutrinos. The top candidate for dark matter, neutrinos are nearly massless subatomic particles that move extremely fast through outer space. Neutrinos are so light and chargeless that they can pass through trillions of miles of matter without interacting with it. The nuclear reactions in stars produce massive amounts of neutrinos. The neutrinos heat the gas around the collapsing stars so much that the supernovas explode.

Neutron. Neutral subatomic particle. The nucleus of an atom consists of neutrons and protons.

Neutron Star. Consisting of a solid mass of neutrons, this supernova explosion remnant is a collapsed star up to fifteen miles across. An amount of neutron star the size of a sugar cube weighs about 100 million tons: The star is extremely dense and compact, with no empty space. A really large neutron star might collapse and turn into a black hole.

Night Ghasts. In Lyra's world, these ghostly horrors visit people in the night.

Northern Lights. See Aurora Borealis.

Oracle. A predictive device or entity. A ouija board is an oracle, as are the alethiometer and I Ching.

Parallel Worlds. Alternate, very similar versions of the same world, all of which exist simultaneously.

Photon. A quantum or particle of light.

Plasma. We all know that ice is a solid, water is a liquid, and steam is a gas. More diffuse than ordinary gas, plasma is used in man-made devices such as neon lights, mercury-vapor lamps, and various types of laboratory equipment. It's estimated that 99.9 percent of all matter in the universe exists in the plasma state. Because the solar plasma is intimately connected to the Northern Lights, and because the Northern Lights are integral to the ideas of dark matter (aka Dust) and dark energy, which make up 90–95 percent of the mass of the universe, the brilliance of *His Dark Materials* is again evident. Could it be that the dark matter/energy is related to the solar plasma and to the Northern Lights? Is it possible that severe disturbances in the Northern Lights could indeed disrupt the dark matter and alter the boundaries between parallel dimensions or worlds? These are all interesting questions posed by Philip Pullman's trilogy, and frankly, today's science just doesn't have the answers: not yet, anyway.

Plenitude. The belief that whatever God could and wanted to do, would be done. The idea that God could have created other worlds with intelligent beings, but that maybe he didn't do it.

Pluralism. The belief that the universe is filled with planets harboring intelligent life.

Polarization. A wavelike property of light related to the particle-like property of the photon's spin. According to Maxwell's equations, a light wave's magnetic and electric fields oscillate at right angles to the direction in which the light is traveling. A photon's polarization refers to the direction in which its electric field is oscillating. Photons can be polarized in many directions, but if a polarizing filter is used (think about sunglasses), the light can be forced into oscillating in specific directions. If a filter is slanted in a particular direction, then the polarization of the photons is slanted in that particular direction.

Quantum Entanglement. In physics, when two things are far apart yet they still know about each other.

Ray. A thin vertical or near-vertical stream of bright Northern Light.

Red Dwarfs. Emitting very little light and slowly contracting over time, red dwarfs are plentiful throughout the universe. Some scientists think that red dwarfs are the most common stars in the universe.

Redshift. A decrease in light frequency from distant galaxies. The decrease appears as a reddening of light. As the universe expands, the redshift may increase.

Schrödinger's Cat Paradox. According to quantum theory, if we put a cat into a box, it may be dead and alive at the same time—until we open the box and observe its condition. How can a cat be dead and alive simultaneously? One answer is that it exists in parallel worlds. This gives rise to the thought that there might be an infinite number of parallel worlds, and in each world we exist in a slightly different way. This is what *His Dark Materials* suggests: that there is an infinite number of parallel worlds, each slightly different from the rest.

Shaman. A spiritual leader and medicine man found throughout the world in ancient times.

Solar System. Our solar system consists of the sun; the nine planets of Mercury, Venus, Earth, Mars, Jupiter, Saturn, Uranus, Neptune, and Pluto; at least six hundred moons; billions of icy comets; and millions of rocky asteroids. The solar system is part of the Milky Way galaxy and is located on a small spiral arm of the Milky Way, which is called the Local or Orion Arm.

Solar Wind. Gas and plasma (protons and electrons) that stream from the sun at 200 to 1,500 kilometers per second (up to 950 miles per second).

Specters. In the bizarre, ancient Mediterranean city called Cittàgazze, deadly specters roam and only children survive. The specters have entered the world of Cittàgazze through holes torn between parallel worlds, and they basically suck the life out of adults.

Star. As hydrogen and other gases collapse due to gravitational forces, atoms collide at increasing speeds and the gas gets very hot. Eventually, the gas is so hot that the hydrogen atoms no longer bounce off each other. The hydrogen atoms begin to combine into helium atoms, and as the hydrogen atoms merge, enormous heat is released. The star is born and begins to glow.

String Theory. In this theory, extremely tiny vibrating strings exist, and each type of vibration is related to a subatomic particle. For string theory to work mathematically, there must be ten dimensions, though the most current and advanced version of string theory, called M-Theory, requires eleven dimensions.

Strong Nuclear Force. Holds the nucleus of the atom together. Responsible for most of the matter we see in the visible universe. This is one of the four fundamental forces of the universe.

Supernova. An exploding star that may be so intense it outshines a galaxy.

Super Particles. The theory of supersymmetry indicates that every partner has a super partner with a different spin. For example, electrons and neutrinos, which are types of leptons, have a spin of one-half. The super partners of leptons are called sleptons, and their spins are zero. Super particles are classified as forms of cold dark matter.

Supersymmetry. A part of string theory that suggests that every particle has a super partner with a different spin. Quarks have super partners called squarks with spins of zero. Gluons, which hold the quarks together, have super partners called gluinos. A spin-one photon that causes light has a super partner called a photino.

Trepanning. Process by which a shaman would have a small hole drilled into his skull. It was thought that evil spirits could escape from the hole, leaving the shaman's mind pure enough to help his people; and it was also thought that through the hole, the shaman would be able to communicate more effectively with the cosmic consciousness and good spirits of the universe.

Unified Field Theory. Einstein was seeking this theory, something that would explain all the forces of nature.

Vacuum. The emptiness of outer space, where virtual subatomic particles exist in vast amounts. These virtual particles exist for split seconds before disappearing.

Vampires. They return from the dead, drink your blood, and live forever, unless you find a way to squash them with silver bullets, stakes, and other folkloric methods.

Veil. A total cloudlike covering of Northern Lights.

Warm Dark Matter. A cross between ultra-light hot dark matter neutrinos and slow-moving, heavier cold dark matter WIMPs, this form of dark matter would be like neutrinos with heavier mass.

Wave. A ripple, with light and radio waves being ripples of electromagnetism. Every subatomic particle has a wave associated with it. The wave's function describes the probability of defining the position of the particle.

Weak Nuclear Force. Responsible for radioactive decay, this force isn't strong enough to hold together the nucleus of an atom. It is based on the interactions of neutrinos and electrons. This is one of the four fundamental forces of the universe.

White Dwarfs. Condensed, final versions of small and medium stars, white dwarfs are plentiful throughout the universe. A white dwarf is dim and cool, and has half the sun's mass. It is one of the densest forms of matter.

WIMP. Weakly Interacting Massive Particles; these are exotic subatomic particles such as massive neutrinos, axions, and photinos. Many scientists think that WIMPs, specifically neutrinos, constitute most of the dark matter in the universe.

Witches. Witches play a central role in *His Dark Materials*. More than once, they save Lyra, Will, and their friends. In our world, a witch is somebody who is highly skilled at sorcery and other magical arts. Witches use rituals, spells, herbs, hares, toads, and charms to manipulate nature, people, and inanimate objects. They talk to the spirits, can be invisible, can change shape, and can heal simply by touching the person or animal that is injured. Although witches can be male, most of us think of witches as female.

Wormhole. Multiply connected spaces, passages between universes. It's unknown at this time whether mass can travel through a wormhole without being destabilized or destroyed.

Zombies. Zombies in *His Dark Materials* are people from whom specters have sucked life; they are soulless people, those without human consciousness. In our world, the notion of zombies originated with Haitian Voodoo culture. The word *zombie* comes from the Haitian word *zombi*, which means spirit of the dead. As the story goes, Voodoo priests called *bokors* studied enough black magic to figure out how to resurrect the dead using a powder called *coup padre*. The black magic basically brought a person close to death, then back to life again in a drugged, tranced state so that the zombie staggered around like the walking dead.

BIBLIOGRAPHY

1. What Is *His Dark Materials*?

Philip Pullman, *The Golden Compass: His Dark Materials Book 1*. New York: Alfred A. Knopf, Inc., hardcover, 1996. Originally published as *His Dark Materials I: Northern Lights* in Great Britain by Scholastic Children's Books in 1995. The copy used by author Lois H. Gresh is the trade paperback Borzoi Book published by Alfred A. Knopf, Inc., 2002.

Philip Pullman, *The Subtle Knife: His Dark Materials Book 2*. New York: Alfred A. Knopf, Inc., hardcover, 1997. Originally published in Great Britain by Scholastic Children's Books in 1997. The copy used by author Lois H. Gresh is the trade paperback Borzoi Book published by Alfred A. Knopf, Inc., 2002.

Philip Pullman, *The Amber Spyglass: His Dark Materials Book 3*. New York: Alfred A. Knopf, Inc., hardcover, 2000. Originally published in Great Britain by Scholastic Children's Books in 2000. The copy used by author Lois H. Gresh is the trade paperback Borzoi Book published by Alfred A. Knopf, Inc., 2002.

http://www.randomhouse.com/features/pullman.

Robert McCrum, Guardian Unlimited Books, January 27, 2002, as reported at http://books.guardian.co.uk/whitbread2001/story/0,11169,640032,00.html.

Dave Welch, "Philip Pullman Reaches the Garden," an author interview at http://www.powells.com/authors/pullman.html.

Lili Ladaga, "Philip Pullman Weaves Spell with His Dark Materials," from an author interview by CNN Book News at http://archives.cnn.com/2000/books/news/11/10/philip.pullman.

Philip Pullman, "The Science of Fiction," http://www.hisdarkmaterials.org/.

2. Dust, Dark Matter, Dark Energy, and Other Celestial Things

Milton's *Paradise Lost*, Book Two.

Michael Chabon, "Dust & Daemons," *The New York Review of Books*, March 25, 2004, http://www.nybooks.com/articles/17000.

Sidney van den Bergh, *The Early History of Dark Matter*. The Astronomical Society of the Pacific, June 1999.

Mordehai Milgrom, "Ninety-Five Percent of the Universe Has Gone Missing. Or Has It?" *Scientific American* special report, *Does Dark Matter Really Exist?*, 2003.

James Kaler, *Extreme Stars at the Edge of Creation*. New York: Cambridge University Press, 2001.

Tom Siegfried, *Strange Matters: Undiscovered Ideas at the Frontiers of Space and Time*. Washington, D.C.: Joseph Henry Press, 2002.

Chandra X-ray Observatory, Harvard University. http://chandra.harvard.edu/resources/faq/dmatter/dmatter-12.html.

Brian Greene, *The Fabric of the Cosmos: Space, Time, and the Texture of Reality*. New York: Alfred A. Knopf, 2004.

Chandra X-ray Observatory, Harvard University. http://chandra.harvard.edu/xray astro/dark matter2.html.

http://imagine.gsfc.nasa.gov/docs/dict_ jp.html#neutron_star.

http://imagine.gsfc.nasa.gov/docs/science/know_11/neutron_stars.html.

http://www.astro.ucla.edu/~agm/darkmtr.html.

http://imagine.gsfc.nasa.gov/docs/teachers/galaxies/imagine/page18.html.

Stephen W. Hawking, *The Illustrated Theory of Everything*. Beverly Hills, CA: New Millennium Press, 2003.

L. E. Lewis Jr., *Our Superstring Universe: Strings, Branes, Extra Dimensions, and Superstring-M Theory*. Lincoln, NE: iUniverse, Inc., 2003.

http://chandra.harvard.edu/resources/faq/dmatter/dmatter-19.html.

Michio Kaku and Jennifer Thompson, *Beyond Einstein: The Cosmic Quest for the Theory of the Universe*. New York: Anchor Books, 1995.

Amit Goswami, Richard E. Reed, and Maggie Goswami, *The Self-Aware Universe: How Consciousness Creates the Material World*. New York: Penguin Putnam, 1993.

3. Angels, God, and Paradise

Gustav Davidson, *A Dictionary of Angels, including the Fallen Angels*. New York: The Free Press/Macmillan, Inc., 1967.

The Columbia Encyclopedia, Sixth Edition, 2001, as found at http://www.bartleby.com/65/az/Azrael.html.

"The Belgic Confession of Faith," in *Reformed Confessions of the 16th Century*, A.C. Coleridge, editor. Philadelphia: Westminster, 1966.

Geddes MacGregor, *Angels: Ministers of Grace*. St. Paul, MN: Paragon House Publishers, 1991.

Matthew Fox and Rupert Sheldrake, *The Physics of Angels: Exploring the Realm Where Science and Spirit Meet*. San Francisco: HarperSanFrancisco, 1996.

Peter Kreeft, *Angels (and Demons): What Do We Really Know About Them?* San Francisco: Ignatius Press, 1995.

Michael Shermer, *Why People Believe Weird Things: Pseudoscience, Superstition, and Other Confusions of Our Time*. New York: W.H. Freeman, 1998.

Paul Tillich, *Theology of Culture*. New York: Oxford University Press, 1959.

Michael Jordan, *The Encyclopedia of Gods*. New York: Facts on File, 1993.

Manfred Lurker, *Dictionary of Gods and Goddesses*. New York: Routledge Press, 1987.

David Adams Leeming and Margaret Adams Leeming, *A Dictionary of Creation Myths*. New York: Oxford University Press, 1995.

4. Witches

Kevin Short, "How Witches Fly High." http://www.unsolvedmysteries.com/usm169177.html.

Jani Farrell Roberts, "Did Witches Really Fly?" http://www.witch.plus.com/7day-extracts/witches-flying.html.

Rosemary Ellen Guiley, *The Encyclopedia of Witches & Witchcraft*. New York: Checkmark Books, 1999.

5. Daemons

James Longrigg, *Greek Rational Medicine: Philosophy and Medicine from Alchaeon to the Alexandrians*. New York: Routledge Press, 1993.

Andrew Cunningham, *The Anatomical Renaissance: The Resurrection of the Anatomical Projects of the Ancients*. Aldershot, U.K.: Ashgate, 1997.

New Catholic Encyclopedia. New York: McGraw-Hill, 1967.

G. Ryle, *The Concept of Mind*. New York: Hutchinson, 1949.

6. Parallel Worlds

"Parallel Universes." http://www.bbc.co.uk/science/horizon/2001/paralleluni.shtml.

Max Tegmark, *Parallel Universes*. www.sciam.com, 2003.

Neil de Grasse Tyson and Donald Goldsmith, *Origins: Fourteen Billion Years of Cosmic Evolution*. New York: W.W. Norton & Company, 2004.

Marcus Chown, "It Came from Another Dimension." *New Scientist*, December 2004.

New Scientist, March 16, 2002.

Michio Kaku, *Parallel Worlds*. New York: Doubleday, January 2005.

Lois H. Gresh and Robert Weinberg, "Crisis on Infinite Earths" in *The Science of Supervillains*. New York: John Wiley & Sons, Inc., 2004.

http://www.nationmaster.com/encyclopedia/Copenhagen-interpretation.

Tim Appenzeller, "Someplace Like Earth." *National Geographic*, December 2004.

Lois Gresh and Robert Weinberg, *The Science of Superheroes*. New York: John Wiley & Sons, 2002.

Frank Drake, forword to *Sharing the Universe*, by Seth Shostak. Berkeley, CA: Berkeley Hills Books, 1998.

Peter F. Ward and Donald Brownlee, *Rare Earth*. New York: Copernicus, 2000.

David Darling, *Life Everywhere: The Maverick Science of Astrobiology*. New York: Basic Books, 2001.

Interview with Michio Kaku. *Astrobiology Magazine*, April 26, 2004, at http://www.astrobio.net/news.

7. The Afterlife: Hell, Harpies, and Heaven

Richard Barber and Anne Riches, *Dictionary of Fabulous Beasts*. United Kingdom: Boydell Press, 2000.

1 Samuel 28:7.

Job 14:21; also Isaiah 63:16.

Alice K. Turner, *The History of Hell*. New York: Harcourt Brace & Company, 1993.

8. Specters, Vampires, Night Ghasts, and Zombies

Sandy Peterson, *Field Guide to Cthulhu Monsters: A Field Observer's Handbook of Preternatural Entities*. Hayward, California: Chaosium, Inc., 1988.

9. Aurora Borealis (Northern Lights)

Harald Falck-Ytter, *Aurora: The Northern Lights in Mythology, History, and Science*, originally published in Germany, 1983; paperback English edition, New York: Bell Pond Books, 1999.

Fridtjof Nansen, *Furthest North*. London: Constable, 1904. In Falck-Ytter.

Robert F. Scott, *Scott's Last Expedition*. London: Murray, 1927. In Falck-Ytter.

R. H. Eather, *Majestic Lights*. Washington, D.C.: American Geophysical Union, 1980.

Lucy Jago, *The Northern Lights: The True Story of the Man Who Unlocked the Secrets of the Aurora Borealis*. New York: Alfred A. Knopf, Inc., 2001.

http://www.northern-lights.no/.

Candace Savage, *Aurora: The Mysterious Northern Lights*. Buffalo, NY: Firefly Books, 2001.

George Bryson, *Northern Lights: The Science, Myth, and Wonder of the Aurora Borealis*. Seattle: Sasquatch Books, 2001.

10. Weird Science, Part 1

"Quantum Entanglement: Going Large." *Nature*, September 27, 2001, as reported at http://www.nature.com/nature/links/010927/010927-2.html.

B. Julsgaard, A. Kozhekin, and E. S. Polzik, "Experimental Long-Lived Entanglement of Two Macroscopic Quantum Objects." *Nature*, Issue 413, 2001.

Peter N. Spotts, "Spooky Action at a Distance." *The Christian Science Monitor*, October 4, 2001. http://www.csmonitor.com/2001/1004/p15s1-stss.html.

George Johnson, *A Shortcut Through Time: The Path to the Quantum Computer*. New York: Alfred A. Knopf, Inc., 2003.

Mark Buchanan, "Quantum Tricks that Read Your Thoughts." *New Scientist*, December 4, 2004. http://www.newscientist.com/channel/fundamentals/quantum-world/.

"Vanderbilt University Engineers Developing Robotic Insects," http://www.robotbooks.com/robot-insects.htm.

Leonard David, "Flapping Robotic Insects Could Extend Range of Rover Missions," http://www.space.com/scienceastronomy/solarsystem/mars flapper 011205-1.html.

Chris Riley, "Robotic Insect Takes to the Air." *BBC News*, http://news.bbc.co.uk/1/hi/sci/tech/1270306.stm.

R. Colin Johnson, "Flying Robotic Insect Slated to Explore Mars." *EE Times*, http://www.eet.com/story/OEG20020114S0081.

Kevin Bonsor, "How Spy Flies Will Work." http://science.howstuffworks.com/spy-fly1.htm.

Ivan Noble, "Robot Insect Walks on Water." *BBC News*, http://news.bbc.co.uk/1/hi/sci/tech/3126299.stm.

"Insect-Based Robots to Fly like Magic." *ABC News Online*, August 2004, http://www.abc.net.au/science/news/scitech/SciTechRepublish_1181486.htm.

Jonathan Gravenor, "Bee Robotics." January 2004, http://www.xposed.com/gadgets/bee robotics.aspx.

http://www.ciderpresspottery.com/ZLA.html.

http://spot.colorado.edu/~dziadeck/zf/introduction.htm.

http://www.airships.net/.

http://www.geocities.com/CapeCanaveral/Launchpad/2899/gyrotech.html.

http://www.indoorduration.com/williamschapter1.htm.

http://www.unc.edu/%7Efranco/autogyro/physics.html.

11. Weird Science, Part 2

Hellmut Wilhelm and Richard Wilhelm, *Understanding the I Ching: The Wilhelm Lectures on the Book of Changes*. Princeton, NJ: Princeton University Press, 1995.

Richard Wilhelm and Cary F. Baynes, *The I Ching or Book of Changes*. Princeton, NJ: Princeton University Press, 1977; original copyright 1950 by Bollingen Foundation, Inc., New York.

Mirfatykh Z. Zakiev, "Ethnic Roots of the Tatar People." http://www.hun-magyar.org/tatar/tatar-origin.html.

Mircea Eliade, *Shamanism: Archaic Techniques of Ecstasy*. Princeton, NJ: Princeton University Press, 1964.

Michael Harner, *The Way of the Shaman*. New York: HarperCollins, 1980.

http://en.wikipedia.org/wiki/Attila the Hun.

Lois Gresh and Robert Weinberg, *The Science of Superheroes*. New York: John Wiley & Sons, 2002.